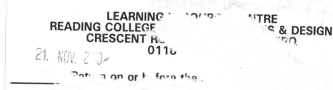
Practise Your
Modal Verbs

Mike Watkins

Series editor: Donald Adamson

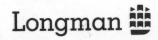
Longman

Longman Group UK Limited,
Longman House, Burnt Mill, Harlow,
Essex CM20 2JE, England
and Associated Companies throughout the world.

First published 1990
Third impression 1991

Set in 10/12pt Linotron Century light

Produced by Longman Singapore Publishers Pte Ltd
Printed in Singapore

ISBN 0 582 00993 6

Illustrated by Norah Fitzwater,
David Parkins and Chris Ryley

Contents

Introduction

Answer key

Introduction

1 What are modal verbs?

They are AUXILIARY verbs which:
a) go before *not* in negative sentences (e.g. He *would not* come)
b) go before the SUBJECT in interrogative sentences (e.g. *May I* come?)
c) go before forms of *be* and *have* in compound tenses (e.g. He *may be* coming or He *may have* come)
d) do not have INFINITIVE or GERUND forms (we cannot say *to must* or *mighting*)

2 List of modals

Affirmative		Negative	
Full	*Reduced*	*Full*	*Reduced*
will	'll	will not	won't
would	'd	would not	wouldn't
shall	–	shall not	shan't
should	–	should not	shouldn't
can	–	cannot	can't
could	–	could not	couldn't
may	–	may not	–
might	–	might not	mightn't
must	–	must not	mustn't
ought to	–	ought not to	oughtn't to
need*	–	need not	needn't

* *Need* can also be used as a full verb. It can only be used as a modal in NEGATIVE or INTERROGATIVE sentences, e.g.

      i) *You needn't do it.*
OR ii) *You don't need to do it.* (both are equally common)

      iii) *Need I do it?*
OR iv) *Do I need to do it?* (iii is less common than iv)

Dare can also be used as a modal in NEGATIVE and INTERROGATIVE sentences, usually when the subject is *I* or *we*. However, as its meaning is quite different from that of the other modals, it is not included in this book.

3 Modal constructions (using *will* for examples)

1	subject + full modal + verb	*It will be difficult.*
2	subject + reduced modal + verb	*It'll be difficult.*
3	subject + full modal + *not* + verb	*It will not be difficult.*
4	subject + reduced negative modal + verb	*It won't be difficult.*
5	full modal + subject + verb	*Will it be difficult?*
6	full modal + subject + *not* + verb	*Will it not be difficult?*
7	reduced negative modal + subject + verb	*Won't it be difficult?*
8	*Wh-* + full modal + subject + verb	*Who will you ask?*
9	*Wh-* + reduced modal + subject + verb	*Who'll you ask?*
10	subject + full modal	*Yes, I will.*
11	subject + full modal + *not*	*No, I will not.*
12	subject + reduced negative modal	*No, I won't.*
13	full modal + subject	*Will it?*
14	reduced negative modal + subject	*Won't it?*

4 Tag questions

A very common pattern in spoken English is STATEMENT + TAG QUESTION:

You're English, *aren't you*? (main clause POSITIVE, tag question NEGATIVE)
This radio doesn't work, *does it?* (main clause NEGATIVE, tag question POSITIVE)

If there is a MODAL in the main clause, it is used in the tag question (although *may* is not normally used in tag questions):

You'*ll* get angry, *won't you*?
You *won't* get angry, *will you*?

This plant *should* be watered every day, *shouldn't it*?
Records *shouldn't* be left in the sun, *should they*?

There *could* have been an accident, *couldn't there*?
John *can't* have got our letter, *can he*?

Their plane *ought* to have landed by now, *oughtn't it*?
We *oughtn't* to have done that, *ought we*?

Your mother *might* have put it there, *mightn't she*?

I *needn't* go yet, *need I*?

1 *Will* and *Would* 1 – future and reported speech

1 Stephen and Julie Wilson are planning a party, but their parents are a little worried. Choose phrases from the speech bubbles to complete the conversations:

> *Will there be …?*
> *Won't there be …?*

> *There'll be …*
> *There won't be …*

MR WILSON: How many people ¹ *will there be* at the party?

JULIE: Oh, ² _____ about 15, I expect.

MR WILSON: What ³ _____ to eat? No hot dogs, I hope! They make a mess.

JULIE: No, Dad, ⁴ _____ any hot dogs.

⁵ _____ hamburgers.

MRS WILSON: I'm worried about the neighbours. ⁶ _____ too much noise?

STEPHEN: Well, ⁷ _____ a bit of noise, but ⁸ _____ too much.

2

You'll clear up afterwards, *won't you?*	Yes, *we will.*
It *won't* be noisy, *will it?*	No, *it won't.*

Complete in the same way, using *'ll, will, won't:*

1 'You *won't* make a mess, *will you* ?'   'No, *we won't* .'

2 'The party _____ be finished by 11, _____ ?'   'Yes, _____ .'

3 'There _____ be any food dropped, _____ ?'   'No, _____ .'

4 'People _____ be careful with the glasses, _____ ?'   'Yes, _____ .'

3

Will → *Would*	
Won't → *Wouldn't*	in reported speech

Mr and Mrs Wilson's fears were justified:

1 'You said it *wouldn't be* noisy!'

2 'You said the party _____ by 11!'

3 'You said people _____ with the glasses!'

4 'You said there _____ any food dropped!'

4 *Will* is often used when MAKING DECISIONS. Complete the conversation below, using words from the table:

I'll/we'll I/we won't will you	have

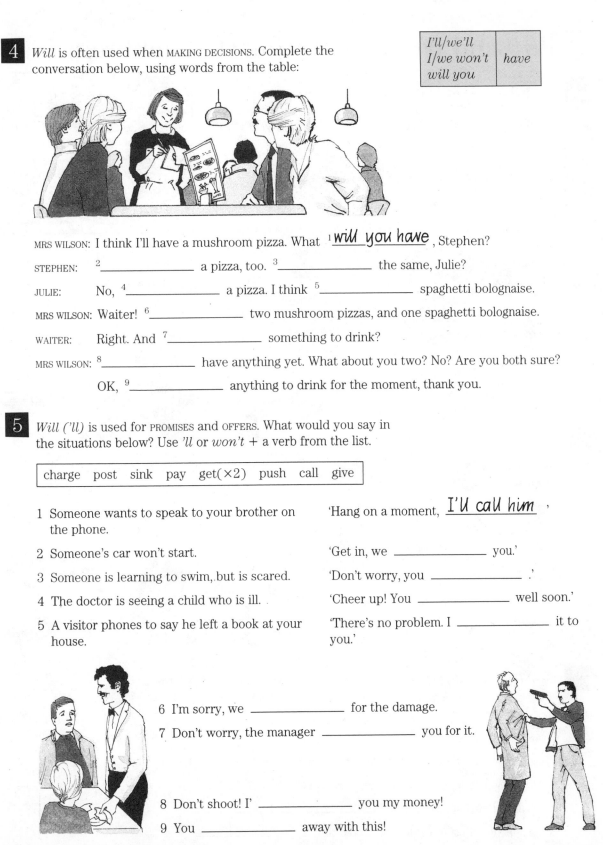

MRS WILSON: I think I'll have a mushroom pizza. What ¹*will you have* , Stephen?

STEPHEN: ²_____ a pizza, too. ³_____ the same, Julie?

JULIE: No, ⁴_____ a pizza. I think ⁵_____ spaghetti bolognaise.

MRS WILSON: Waiter! ⁶_____ two mushroom pizzas, and one spaghetti bolognaise.

WAITER: Right. And ⁷_____ something to drink?

MRS WILSON: ⁸_____ have anything yet. What about you two? No? Are you both sure?

            OK, ⁹_____ anything to drink for the moment, thank you.

5 *Will* (*'ll*) is used for PROMISES and OFFERS. What would you say in the situations below? Use *'ll* or *won't* + a verb from the list.

charge   post   sink   pay   get(×2)   push   call   give

1 Someone wants to speak to your brother on the phone.

'Hang on a moment, *I'll call him* ,'

2 Someone's car won't start.

'Get in, we _____ you.'

3 Someone is learning to swim, but is scared.

'Don't worry, you _____ .'

4 The doctor is seeing a child who is ill.

'Cheer up! You _____ well soon.'

5 A visitor phones to say he left a book at your house.

'There's no problem. I _____ it to you.'

6 I'm sorry, we _____ for the damage.

7 Don't worry, the manager _____ you for it.

8 Don't shoot! I' _____ you my money!

9 You _____ away with this!

Will and *Would* 2 – requesting and refusing

1 Asking people to do things (informal style)

Will you is very direct – almost an order; *Would you* is more polite:

Would you help me carry this, please?
Will you help me carry it NOW – I'm dropping it!

Complete the dialogues with suitable requests, using *Will* or *Would*:

1 MR WILSON: Stephen, **would you** clean up the mess in the kitchen?

STEPHEN: Later. I'm tired.

2 MR WILSON: _____ do it NOW, please!

3 STEPHEN: Julie, your radio's very loud.

_____ turn it down, please?

4 STEPHEN: Can't you hear me, Julie?

_____ turn your radio down! I'm trying to study.

2 *Would you mind (not)...-ing* is more formal. It often indicates that the speaker is rather angry, or that he feels he has the **right** to make the request:

Would you mind shutting the door, please?
Would you mind not doing that?

Changing words where necessary, write what you would say to someone who ...

1 is smoking, in a no-smoking area: _____

2 is talking during a concert: _____

3 has opened a train window on a cold day: _____

3 *Won't* (past = *wouldn't*) is used when a person, or an object, **persists** in not doing something you want him (or it) to do.

> This box is really heavy – it *won't* move.   (= NO ONE CAN MOVE IT)
> The rain went on and on – it *wouldn't* stop. (= IT 'REFUSED' TO STOP)

The first time Mr and Mrs Wilson went abroad, they were on their honeymoon – lots of things went wrong. They still laugh about it, though at the time it was not so funny! Look at the pictures, and complete Mrs Wilson's description of it to her children with *won't* or *wouldn't* and these verbs:

> accept/let/light/move/start/stay/stop

'We were going to leave at 6 am on the day after our wedding, to get the 9 o'clock ferry from Dover to France. Then the first thing went wrong – the car ¹ _wouldn't_ _start_ ! Dad got quite angry, and kept shouting: "WHY ² _____ it _____ ?" In the end he had to call a garage, and the mechanic wanted £20. We'd changed all our money into foreign currency, and in those days people ³ _____ normally _____ cheques from someone they didn't know.

   "What shall I do?" Dad cried. "He ⁴ _____ _____ a cheque!" At last the mechanic agreed, and we just got to Dover in time for the boat.'

'And why ⁵ _____ the car _____ ?' asked Stephen. 'Your Dad had forgotten to buy petrol', Mrs Wilson replied.

'Anyway, we got to a campsite in France and tried to put up our tent, but it was so windy that it ⁶ _____ _____ up. We ended up sleeping in the car. Next morning, we found that all our cooking things were wet. "The stove ⁷ _____ _____ !" your Dad kept saying. So, we had a cold breakfast!

   But the funniest thing was a few days later, when we were in the mountains. There was a flock of sheep in the road, and they ⁸ _____ _____ us pass. "Sheep ⁹ _____ _____ unless you make a loud noise!" Dad said, and he pressed the horn. But the horn got stuck, and it ¹⁰ _____ _____ ! It was terribly embarrassing, but at least the sheep got out of our way!'

3 *Will* and *Would* 3 – conditionals

1 *Will* is used in the main clause of first conditionals (to make predictions about situations that are **likely** to occur) – the verb in the *if* clause is PRESENT:

It'll go bad *if you leave* it out of the fridge. (= SO DON'T DO IT!)

Would is used in second conditionals, where the situation is **unlikely**, *but possible*. The verb in the *if* clause is PAST:

It'd go bad *if you left* it out of the fridge. (= I KNOW YOU ARE NOT LIKELY TO DO THAT.)

Complete the dialogue below with a pronoun + *'ll/will/won't/'d/wouldn't*:

¹ **They'll** probably go away if we don't make any noise.

²_____ only harm us if they're frightened. If my brother was here, ³_____ want to shoot them. ⁴_____ certainly attack us if we did that. He's not a good shot – ⁵_____ probably _____ hit them. ⁶_____ _____ get angry if I film them, do you think?

2 *'ll (will)* is used in 'hidden' conditionals (when the *if* clause is **implied**) – for example, in warnings and threats. *'d (would)* is used when you **report** the warning – e.g. to remind the person of the warning you gave. Use *'ll/won't/would/'d/wouldn't*, and a verb from the list, to complete these warnings and threats:

wake get catch go burn cut call

1 Mind how you open that tin – you' **'ll cut** yourself!

   (later) I told you you' **'d cut** if you weren't careful!

2 Don't let the baby play on the floor – he' _____ dirty!

   (later) I told you the baby _____ if you let him play on the floor!

3 They must leave by 9 o'clock or they _____ their flight!

   (later) I told you they _____ if they didn't leave by nine!

4 Tell her not to touch that saucepan – she' _____ herself!

   (later) I warned you she' _____ if she _____ !

5 Do your homework now or we _____ to the cinema!

   (later) I told you we _____ if you _____ .

6 Don't let the children make a noise – they' _____ the baby!

   (later) I kept telling you the children _____ the baby if they _____ .

3 *Would have* is used for possibilities in the past which did not become reality (third conditionals). The verb in the *if* clause is PAST PERFECT:

I wouldn't have come if I'd known that.

Mr Wilson made a list of things to do over the weekend. At the end of the weekend, he looked through the list, making comments on what he *had* or *hadn't* done. Use *'d/would/ wouldn't (have)* to fill the blanks:

I didn't manage to cut the grass, but I ¹ __would have__ done it

if it hadn't rained all the time. I didn't paint the door either – it

probably ² _____ dried in this weather, ³ _____

it? I repaired the television, though. There was a football match

on, and Stephen ⁴ _____ been very disappointed if I hadn't,

⁵ _____ he? I didn't manage to hang the pictures, I'm afraid, but I

⁶ _____ if I'd found some nails. It's a good thing I got money from the cash

machine – there ⁷ _____ been enough for the shopping if I hadn't,

⁸ _____ there?

THINGS TO DO
cut grass
paint door
mend TV
hang pictures
Get cash !

4 **Second and third conditionals mixed (including *implied* conditions)**

Complete the dialogue with *would(n't)* or *would(n't) have.* Use abbreviated forms where possible.

I ¹ __wouldn't__ wear clothes like that!

Ah! But I expect you ² _____ done

when you were younger,

³ _____ you?

Gosh! Did you see that? It

⁴ _____ happened if the lorry hadn't

stopped suddenly, ⁵ _____ it?

No, the Mini ⁶ _____ stopped in

time. I ⁷ _____ be furious if it

happened to me, ⁸ _____ you?

Yes, I ⁹ _____ . But there

probably ¹⁰ _____ been an accident

at all if that child hadn't suddenly crossed the

road, ¹¹ _____ there?

4 *Will* and *Would* 4 – other uses

1 Making inferences – *will('ll)* and *won't* + *be* or *have*

He won't be home yet.	It's almost certain he isn't home yet.
He'*ll* still *be* working.	It's almost certain he's still working.
He'*ll have* the result by now.	It's almost certain he has the result by now.
He *won't have* got our letter yet.	It's almost certain he hasn't received it yet.

What does Mr Wilson say in the situations below? Complete the sentences using items from the box:

woken up yet	for one of the children	changed
your great grandmother	the postman	getting worried

1 He hears a knock at the door: Ah! <u>*That'll be the postman.*</u>

2 The phone rings at midnight: I'm not getting up! It _____

3 Stephen's friend calls at 7am: It's very early. He _____

4 He and his wife are delayed in town: The children _____

5 Stephen and Julie are looking through old photos with him: That _____

6 He is going to meet his old teacher, after 20 years: I expect he _____

2 Wishes

I wish Stephen *would* tidy his room.
I wish he *wouldn't* leave his clothes on the floor.

Mrs Wilson sometimes feels that the children don't help enough. Today, for example:

Stephen left his wet towel on the bed.	Stephen left his muddy shoes on the carpet.
Julie didn't make her bed.	Somebody had spilt coffee on the tablecloth.
Stephen didn't turn off his light.	Nobody had offered to wash up.

Write what she said about each annoying thing, using *would* or *wouldn't*:

1 I wish Stephen <u>*wouldn't leave his wet towel on the bed*</u> !

2 I wish Julie _____ !

3 I wish Stephen _____ !

4 I wish Stephen _____ !

5 I wish people _____ !

6 I wish somebody _____ !

3 *Would like* and *Would rather* – wants and preferences in the present

I'd like to Would you like to	go have etc.

I'd rather I'd rather not Would you rather	go have etc.

Rewrite the following as direct speech, using the forms above:

Julie asked her aunt what she wanted to drink. She asked her if she would prefer tea or coffee. Her aunt said she would prefer tea. Julie then asked her cousins if they wanted tea, but they said they would prefer coffee. Then Julie asked if Amanda, the baby, wanted anything, but her aunt said Amanda would prefer not to have anything at the moment, as she would prefer to sleep.

JULIE: What ¹ *would you like to* drink, Auntie? ² _____ have tea or coffee?

AUNT: I ³_____ have tea, please.

JULIE: What about you two boys. ⁴ _____ have tea as well?

BOYS: No, we ⁵_____ coffee, please.

JULIE: OK. And what about Amanda? ⁶ _____ to drink something?

AUNT: No, I think she ⁷ _____ have anything at the moment.

She ⁸_____ sleep!

4 Regrets about the past

I'd like to I'd rather (not)	have	gone etc.

The Wilsons' neighbours recently went to the USA for a holiday, but they weren't entirely satisfied. Rewrite these sentences, using the forms above (with appropriate subjects):

1 Mr Green wanted to see a baseball game, but didn't.

He'd 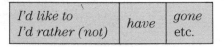 *like to have seen* a baseball game.

2 Mrs Green didn't enjoy travelling around by bus.

She'd _____ travelled around by bus.

3 They went in winter, but summer would have been better.

They'd _____ in summer than in winter.

4 They all agreed that it was a bad idea to go by ship.

They'd _____ gone by ship.

5 *Shall*

1 Future

I shall and *We shall* are often used in formal written English instead of *I'll (I will)* and *We'll (We will)*. (*Shall* is **not** normally used with other subjects.)

INFORMAL:	I'll be pleased to accept your invitation.
FORMAL:	I *shall* be pleased to accept your invitation.
INFORMAL:	I'm afraid we *won't* have reached a decision by then.
FORMAL:	I am afraid we *shall not* have reached a decision by then.

At work, Mr Wilson often telephones people to tell them something, then writes to confirm it. Today he has bad news for a customer:

Now complete the letter of confirmation which he wrote. Use *I* or *We shall (not)* – or *will* if the subject is **not** *I* or *we*.

Dear Mr Johnson,

       I am sorry to inform you that because of a problem at the factory we ¹___*shall not*___ have your order ready on time. However, we ²_____ _____ by the end of the month, and I ³_____ sure that there are no more delays. I am afraid that ⁴_____ for the next fortnight, as ⁵_____ on holiday. However, my assistant John Smith ⁶_____ here, and I am sure that ⁷_____ any further problems. I hope that ⁸_____ to meet when I get back.

    I apologise once again for this delay.

              Yours sincerely,

              S. Wilson

Hello, is that Mr Johnson? Wilson here. Look, I'm terribly sorry, but there's been a bit of a problem at the factory. Yes, and we won't have your order ready on time, I'm afraid. We'll do our best to send it off by the end of the month . . .

Yes, of course . . . I understand. I'll make sure there aren't any more delays. I'm afraid I won't be here for the next couple of weeks, I'll be on holiday . . . but don't worry, John Smith will be here and I'm sure there won't be any more problems.

. . . Well, nice to talk to you. Perhaps we'll be able to meet when I get back. I'm terribly sorry about the delay, again. Goodbye, then.

2 Suggestions

Shall I/we... is a common way of making suggestions. With this meaning, it is not at all formal:

Shall we invite the Johnsons to dinner?
Shall I lay the table?

When the Wilsons gave a dinner party for Mr and Mrs Johnson, not everything went as planned. Complete the suggestions:

1

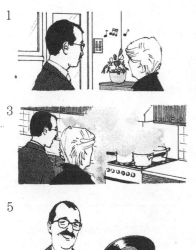

2

Shall	I we	listen to answer get you turn on take open	the window? the light? the door? another glass? some music? your coat?

1 <u>Shall I answer the door?</u>

2 _____

3 _____

4 _____

5 _____

6 _____

3

5

4

6

3

Shall is also used informally in questions that ask for INSTRUCTIONS. Stephen and Julie cleared up next morning, but they kept asking what to do. Write their questions:

How Where	shall	I we	clean remove sweep up put put away	this broken glass? these flowers? this pan? the tablecloth? these stains?

1 <u>How shall I clean this pan?</u>   'With a rough cloth.'

2 _____ we _____? 'In a vase.'

3 _____ I _____? 'With a brush!'

4 _____ we _____? 'In the drawer.'

5 _____ I _____

_____? 'With stain-remover.'

6 *Should* and *Ought to* 1 – advice and criticism

1 We often see people doing things we consider wrong, and we want to advise them, or talk critically about them to others. For example:

You *should* work harder.	He *shouldn't* drive so fast.
You *ought to* be more polite.	They *ought not to* sell these.

Look at the pictures. Beside each one, write something you would say **to** the person, and something **about** the person. Use either *should/shouldn't* or *ought to/ought not to* – there is no difference in meaning, although *should* is perhaps a little more common, and *ought to* a little more emphatic.

1 'You _____ shouldn't eat so much. _____ '

He _____

2 'You _____ '

He _____

3 'You _____ '

He _____

2 Think of three things that people say to you, criticising you. For example:

1 <u>My dentist says I shouldn't eat so many sweets</u>.

2 _____ says I _____

3 _____ says I _____

4 _____ says I _____

3 Now you can criticise somebody you know! For example:

1 <u>Our teacher ought not to give us so much work!</u>

2 _____

3 _____

4 Criticising after the event

Should have ...	Ought to have ...
Shouldn't have ...	Ought not to have ...

Stephen's football team, Brightsmouth, have lost 3–1. Stephen thinks they lost because:

– Bob Hacker didn't play.
– The goalkeeper tried to stop their first goal with his foot.
– The fans started booing in the second half.
– Brightsmouth weren't given a penalty.
– The team didn't try hard enough.
– Nobody was watching the Mancastle number 10.
– Brightsmouth's first goal was disallowed.

Complete Stephen's criticism, using each construction in the box at least once:

1 Bob Hacker ____*should have*____ played.

2 The goalkeeper _____ to stop their first goal with his foot.

3 The fans _____ in the second half.

4 Brightsmouth _____ a penalty.

5 The team _____ harder.

6 Somebody _____ the Mancastle number 10.

7 Brightsmouth's first goal _____ disallowed.

5 Mixed criticism and strong advice

Mr Wilson is not a very patient driver. He often has arguments with other people on the road:

'You *shouldn't* have been going so fast!'
'You *ought to* look in your mirror sometimes!'

Use the appropriate phrase with *should* or *ought to*, to complete what he said when.....

1 He bumped into the car in front. 'You ___*shouldn't have/ ought not to have*___ been going so slowly!'

2 The car in front turned unexpectedly. 'You _____ signal when

you're going to turn!'

3 Someone was coming the wrong way down a one-way street.

'You _____ be coming in this direction.'

4 He nearly hit a car without lights. 'You _____ switch on your lights!'

5 He almost ran down a pedestrian. 'You _____ been crossing in the

wrong place!'

6 He ran out of petrol. 'I _____ remembered to fill up the tank!'

7 *Should* and *Ought to* 2 – contrasted with *had better*; future probability

1 *Had better*

You'*d better* drive carefully – there's a police car behind us!
We'*d better not* go to bed too late, had we? We've got to leave early tomorrow.

Had better or *'d better* is often used in conversation to give advice about what **should** be done in the future, **in order to avoid some bad consequence**. Complete this conversation with *had better (not)* or *'d better (not)*:

MRS WILSON: Did you remember to pay the phone bill?

MR WILSON: No, I completely forgot. We ¹ *'d better* pay it soon, or they'll cut us off! Well, it's 8.20 – I ²_____ leave for work.

MRS WILSON: It's raining, you know – you ³_____ go out without a coat.

MR WILSON: You're right. How's Stephen's knee this morning, by the way?

MRS WILSON: Still hurting. He ⁴_____ play football, had he?

MR WILSON: No, I don't think he ⁵_____ . He'd only make it worse. Oh, I nearly forgot – did you get any petrol yesterday?

MRS WILSON: No, you ⁶_____ get some soon – the tank's nearly empty.

MR WILSON: Right, I will. See you later, then!

2 Contrast of *should/ought* and *had better*

Complete the sentences about the people in the pictures. Use phrases containing *had better* or *'d better* where possible. Otherwise use *should/ought to*.

A

He ¹ *should have / ought to have* got up earlier. By ten to nine, he

²_____ been walking to the station, not still eating his breakfast. And since he was late getting up, he

³_____ had such a big breakfast. He really

⁴_____ been surprised to see he had missed the

train, ⁵_____ he? Tomorrow he ⁶_____

get up at eight o'clock, ⁷_____ he?

Those children [1] __*shouldn't have/ ought not to have*__ been playing near the river in the first place, [2] _____ ? Someone [3] _____ been looking after them. Young children [4] _____ be supervised if there is any danger. This is what the policeman thought, too: 'You [5] _____ take more care of them in future, [6] _____ you!'

'Oh dear! We [1] _____ eaten so much, [2] _____ ? We [3] _____ come here again, [4] _____ we? This restaurant really is very expensive – they [5] _____ charge extra for each vegetable. All the prices [6] _____ be clearly displayed outside the restaurant, [7] _____ ?'

3 *Should* and *ought to* can indicate FUTURE PROBABILITY (especially of something the speaker **wants**).
Stephen's football team, Brightsmouth, have reached the semi-final of the cup. Here are the semi-final matches:

Brightsmouth vs Mancastle
Wetford vs Liverton

Stephen and his father are looking at the league table, and trying to predict who will be in the final. Complete their conversation with *should/shouldn't* or *ought (not) to/oughtn't to*:

Points	
Brightsmouth	42
Mancastle	36
Liverton	27
Wetford	26

STEPHEN: Brightsmouth [1] __*should*__ beat Mancastle.

DAD: I agree, they [2] _____ lose that match.

STEPHEN: How about the other semi-final? Liverton [3] _____ beat Wetford, [4] _____ they?

DAD: Yes, they [5] _____ , but it won't be easy.

STEPHEN: If Brightsmouth reach the final, they [6] _____ win the cup. They [7] _____ have much difficulty against either Wetford or Liverton.

8 *Can* and *Could* 1 – skill and achievement

1 *Can* and *Can't* – present skill

How well *can* you speak Spanish?
I *can* read it quite well, but I *can't* speak it very well.

Julie is applying for a job with an international
company, and has given a self-assessment of her
skill in foreign languages. This is what she put:

	1 = hardly at all
	2 = not very well
	3 = quite well
	4 = very well

	French	German	Portuguese
Reading	4	3	3
Writing	3	2	2
Listening	2	1	2
Speaking	3	2	1

This means that:

1 She __can__ read French very well, but she
   __can't__ understand it very well when it is spoken.

2 She _____ read Portuguese _____ _____ , but she
   _____ hardly speak it at all.

3 She _____ speak German _____ _____ , but she
   _____ read it _____ _____ .

4 She _____ speak French _____ _____ , but she
   _____ speak German so well.

5 She can't speak _____ as well as she can _____ it.

6 She _____ _____ all three languages better than she
   _____ _____ them when they are spoken.

2 *Could* and *Couldn't* – skill in the past

A year ago, Julie could hardly speak French at all, but **now**
she can speak it quite well!

What about you? Write a sentence about your English **in the
past**, and **now**. Then two more true sentences about other skills
(e.g. swimming, driving):

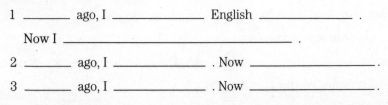

1 _____ ago, I _____ English _____ .

   Now I _____ .

2 _____ ago, I _____ . Now _____ .

3 _____ ago, I _____ . Now _____ .

3 ***'ll be able to* and *Won't be able to* – skill and achievement in the future**

> I can't use modal verbs very well yet, but soon I'*ll be able to* use them perfectly.
> (= SKILL IN THE FUTURE)
>
> If you learn these pages you'*ll be able to* answer all the questions in the exam next week.
> (= ACHIEVEMENT IN THE FUTURE)
>
> (Note that *can* is also possible for ACHIEVEMENT IN THE FUTURE, but is less precise in meaning.)

Complete these sentences about the Wilson's plans with *can/can't* (= PRESENT SKILL)
and '*ll be able to/won't be able to* (= FUTURE SKILL OR ACHIEVEMENT):

1 Mr Wilson is taking a course in Computer Programming. At the moment he __can't__
 write complicated programs, but soon __he'll be able to__ write them quite well.

2 Mrs Wilson is learning Spanish. She _____ speak it very well yet. She
 hopes she _____ to by the end of the course.

3 Stephen is taking guitar lessons. He _____ play quite well already, but he
 hopes he _____ play like a professional if he continues with his lessons.

4 Julie is taking a typing course. She knows she _____ pass her secretarial
 exams next year unless she improves her typing speed. She's doing well, and soon
 she _____ 60 words a minute.

4 ***Was able to* – achievement in the past**

> | *Could* | = HAD THE ABILITY (including + verbs of perception: *see, hear,* etc.) |
> | *Couldn't* | = DIDN'T HAVE THE ABILITY or FAILED TO/DIDN'T MANAGE TO |
> | *Was/were able to* | = MANAGED TO (on a particular occasion) |

Stephen *was able to* climb it, but Julie *couldn't* climb it without help

Complete the account of the climb with *could/couldn't*
wherever possible – otherwise use *was/were able to*:

Stephen and Julie were spending a few days camping with some

friends in Snowdonia. On a climb, there was a difficult section.

Stephen has long arms, and ¹ __was able to__ climb this easily,

but Julie is not so tall and ² _____ reach the hold.

In the end, she ³ _____ reach it by standing on her

friend's shoulders. 'Never mind,' he said. 'I ⁴ _____

get up this bit the first time I tried.' The rest of the climb was

easier, and they ⁵ _____ reach the top by 12 o'clock.

It was warm and sunny, and they ⁶ _____ see the whole of Snowdonia.

Can and Could 2 – possibility

1 Can = 'sometimes' (present); Could = 'sometimes' (past)

The temperature *can* go above 40° in Rio in January.
(= ... 'sometimes' goes above 40° ....)

Mr Wilson is in Rio de Janeiro on business for a few days. A Brazilian friend is showing him round, and tells him what sometimes *happens*, or *used to happen* in the past. Complete each sentence with *can* or *could* + words from the table:

be	difficult /
take	dangerous / cuts /
get	cool / over an hour

1 Be careful when you swim – the sea __can be dangerous__

2 You'd better take a sweater. It _____ at night.

3 There's a tunnel through the mountains now – before it was built, it _____ to get to the other side of the city.

4 The electricity supply is very good now. Years ago there _____ that lasted for hours.

2 Could – possibility in the future

This weather forecaster seems to enjoy being pessimistic. He makes GENERAL STATEMENTS, then gives a *particular warning*. Complete his forecast with *can* or *could*:

Well, when we have a deep area of low pressure near the British Isles at this time of year, winds [1]__can__ be very strong. In fact there [2]_____ be severe gales in some south-western areas. Warm winds [3]_____ sometimes cause avalanches. So, skiers beware! There [4]_____ be dangerous snow conditions this weekend. And further south, the snow is expected to melt fast. A thaw [5]_____ often lead to flooding, and in fact a number of rivers in the west and south [6]_____ rise dangerously in the next 24 hours.

3 *Could, Can't* and *Couldn't* – conclusions

It *could* be true	It's possible that it's true
It *can't* be true	It's not possible that it's true (confident)
It *couldn't* be true	It's not possible that it's true (more tentative)

Note that *can* (positive) is **not** used with this meaning, see *may*, (p. 29).

Mr and Mrs Wilson are reading the newspapers, and commenting on what they read to each other. Complete their conversation with *could/couldn't/can't*:

Listen to this. It says Mancastle [1] *could* go down to Division 2 next year. But that's not possible – they [2]_____ go down unless they lose all their other matches. Well, I suppose that [3]_____ happen, but it's not very likely.

According to this article, there [4]_____ be any other civilisations in the universe – or they'd have contacted us by now. But [5]_____ all those stories of UFOs be true? They [6]_____ be, [7]_____ they? It's possible!

4 Conclusions about the past

He *could have* done it	= IT'S POSSIBLE THAT HE DID IT.	
He *can't have* done it	= IT'S NOT POSSIBLE THAT HE HAS DONE IT. (emphasis on present)	
He *couldn't have* done it	= IT'S NOT POSSIBLE THAT { HE HAS DONE IT.	(less strong, or less
	HE DID IT.	connection with the present)

Note: For conclusions about the past where there is CERTAINTY, see *must have*, (p. 37).

Complete these dialogues:

A Who [1] *could have* built this? The Romans?

The Romans [2]_____ built it, it's too old.

It [3]_____ the Greeks, [4]_____ ?

B Do you think Stephen [1]_____ eaten it?

No, it [2]_____ him, he doesn't like cake.

[3]_____ it _____ been Julie, then?

Yes, that's possible. It [4]_____ her.

10 *Can* and *Could* 3 – permission and requests

1 (P) means 'You *can* park'; (Ⓟ) means 'You *can't* park'. What do these mean?

1 | NO SMOKING | You __can't smoke__ here.

2 | NO ENTRY | You _____ .

3 | MEMBERS ONLY | You _____ only _____ if you are a member.

4 | You _____ go forward, but you _____ .

5 | 6 40° | You _____ it, but you _____ iron it.

6 | MON – SAT 8am–6pm Waiting limited to 1 hour. No return with-in 2 hours. | You _____ park for up to one hour, but you _____ park here again for the next two hours.

2

| *Can/could* | I ask you a question?' |
| | you show me how to use this telephone?' |

Asking permission, or making a request, with *can*, is informal and confident. *Could* is rather more formal, and often more polite. What would you say in the situations below? (Remember that there is only a small difference between *can* and *could* – the manner of the speaker is just as important).

1 To a stranger, if you wanted to know the time.

'Excuse me, __could you__ tell me the time, please?'

2 To your brother, if you wanted him to turn his radio down.

'_____ turn your radio down, please?'

3 To the ticket seller, if you wanted to know the time of the next train.

'_____ me the time of the next train, please?'

4 To the air stewardess, if you wanted some more coffee.

'_____ have some more coffee, please?'

5 To your teacher, if you wanted him/her to help you with a letter.

'_____ help me with this letter, please?'

6 To a shop assistant, if you wanted to try on an article of clothing.

'_____ try this on?'

7 To a waiter, if you wanted the bill.

'_____ have the bill, please?'

3 Very polite ways of asking permission and requesting

Could I possibly interrupt you?
Do you think I could speak to you for a few minutes?
I was wondering if I could ask you for a favour.
I couldn't possibly have another day to finish that work, *could I?*

Could you possibly do me a favour?
Do you think you could help me with a problem I've got?
I was wondering if you could lend me some money for a few days.
You couldn't possibly lend me £20, *could you?*

Study these examples – they are all polite and tentative (although that depends also on the manner of the speaker). Use each form once in the following situations. Use a more direct form in two of them.

1 Mr Wilson asks his boss if he can leave the office an hour earlier than usual.

  <u>Could I possibly leave the office an hour earlier than usual ?</u>

2 Stephen asks his guitar teacher to lend him his guitar for the evening.

_____

3 Mr Wilson wants his neighbour to help him carry a cupboard upstairs.

_____

4 You ask someone to move his car, as it's blocking the entrance to your garage.

_____

5 Julie and two of her friends ask their typing teacher for permission to leave early.

_____

6 Mrs Wilson would like Julie to do some shopping for her, if she has time.

_____

7 You ask a stranger next to you in a train if you can look at his newspaper.

_____

8 You ask your host for permission to use his phone.

_____

9 You ask someone you hardly know for a lift into town.

_____

10 You are checking out of a hotel, and want to pay your bill.

_____

[11] *Could* – unreal and conditional uses

1 After their climb (p. 21), Stephen and his friends were all very *hungry, hot, tired, thirsty,* and *happy*. Use *could* with items in the box to complete their exclamations:

drink 8 bottles of lemonade	eat a kilo of rice
sleep for 24 hours	melt
look at them all day	

STEPHEN: 'I'm so hungry ¹ *I could eat a kilo of rice!* ',

JULIE: 'I'm not hungry, but I'm so thirsty ²_____',

JOHN: 'I didn't sleep well last night. I'm so tired ³_____',

ANNE: 'Me too. And the weather needs to be cooler to climb mountains – I'm so hot

⁴_____',

JULIE: 'The mountains are so beautiful, though. I ⁵_____',

Later, Julie wrote a postcard to her parents, and described how everyone had felt:

Stephen *was* so hungry he *could have eaten* a kilo of rice.

Continue her letter, writing the other sentences in the same way:

I wasn't hungry, but I was so thirsty I ⁶_____ . John and Anne were so tired

they ⁷_____ , and Anne was so hot she ⁸_____ .

The mountains were so beautiful, though. I ⁹_____ .

2 ***I wish I could* – 'impossible' wishes**

Write the most appropriate 'wish' for the people in the sentences below, using the words in the table:

I wish I/we could ...	eat get use understand find afford	the instructions my key a new car cakes dictionaries a job

1 Someone on a diet: '___ *I wish I could eat cakes.* ___',

2 Someone locked out of their house: '_____',

3 Students taking an English exam: '_____',

4 Someone whose car won't start: '_____',

5 An unemployed person '_____',

6 Some people who have just bought a new computer: '_____',

3 **Past possibility – It *didn't* happen, but it *could have done***

Example:

'Hey, that was dangerous – you *could have* got
killed!' (= YOU DIDN'T, BUT IT WAS POSSIBLE)

What *could have* happened in the pictures:

1 You _____ set fire _____

2 The house _____

3 It _____

4 We _____

4 Julie was going to attend an interview for a job. She borrowed
her mother's car, but she had a puncture, and was two hours late
for the interview. Later her mother was rather annoyed.

She thought Julie *could have*:

but Julie said:

– got a lift
– phoned a garage
– walked to the next village
– changed the wheel herself

– she didn't have any tools
– nobody stopped
– it was too far
– there was no phone nearby

Surely you *could have*....., couldn't you? *Couldn't you have*..........?	No, I *couldn't*, because.......! I *could have*, but...........!

Use all four constructions, and the items above, to complete the
dialogue:

1 <u>Couldn't you have got a lift ? I could have but nobody stopped.</u>

2 Surely _____

_____

3 Couldn't _____

_____

4 Surely _____

_____

May and *Might* 1 – permission and possibility

1 Asking permission (formal ways)

(See also pages 24–25.)

'May I....?'	(The speaker is fairly confident that permission will be given – very formal, or ironic!)
'I was wondering if I *might*....' 'Do you think I *might*....?'	(The speaker is less confident – or else being very polite.)

Which forms do you think Mr Wilson would use when...

1 he asks his boss if he can have the afternoon off work:

I was wondering if I might have the afternoon off work.

2 he wants to make a suggestion (at a board meeting):

_____

3 he asks a stewardess on the plane if he can visit the pilot's cabin:

_____

4 Stephen has been using the phone for 20 minutes! Mr Wilson wants to use it:

_____

5 he asks his neighbour if he can borrow his ladder:

_____

2 Formal written regulations

> This book *may be* renewed by post, telephone or personal visit to the library.

Write formal versions, with *may (not)*, of:

1 You can't take dogs into this restaurant.

Dogs **may not be** taken into this restaurant.

2 Children under 12 can't enter unless they're with a grown-up.

Children under 12 _____ enter unless accompanied by an adult.

3 Sorry, we can't sell alcoholic drinks to anyone under 18.

We regret that alcoholic drinks _____ sold to anyone under 18.

4 You can only book a court if you're a member of the tennis club.

Courts _____ only _____ by members of the tennis club.

5 Don't smoke in the classrooms!

Students _____ .

28

3 Present possibility

> *may* = THERE IS A REASONABLE POSSIBILITY
> *might* = THERE IS A POSSIBILITY (BUT NOT A VERY STRONG ONE)

Why isn't Miss Wilson here?

She may be ill – or she might be too nervous. It may not be her fault.

The people interviewing Julie for the job couldn't understand why she was so late. (See p. 27.)

What other possible explanations do the interviewers think of? Use *may/might (not)*:

1 Perhaps her train is late.

Her train may be late.

2 Perhaps she doesn't know the way.

_____

3 It's just possible she thinks it's on another day.

_____

4 Perhaps there's a traffic jam.

_____

5 Maybe she feels the salary is too low.

_____

6 There's a slight possibility that she doesn't want the job after all.

_____

7 Perhaps she's not feeling well today.

_____

8 It's just possible she has a good reason.

_____

4 Future possibility

> He *should* pass. = I THINK HE'LL PASS, BUT IT'S NOT CERTAIN.
> He *may (not)* pass. = THERE'S A REASONABLE POSSIBILITY THAT HE WILL/WON'T PASS.
> He *might (not)* pass. = THERE'S SOME POSSIBILITY THAT HE WILL/WON'T PASS.

Stephen is taking exams next term, and Mr and Mrs Wilson are talking to his headmaster at a teacher-parent meeting. Complete his comments with *should, may (not)* or *might (not)*:

He's doing quite well in English, and he ¹ __should__ pass without any

difficulty. He ² _____ even pass with distinction if he tries very

hard. His Maths is not so good – he ³ _____ even fail, though I

don't think that's very likely. His Chemistry teacher isn't too happy with

him, and says Stephen ⁴ _____ pass. He doesn't seem to show any

interest in the subject, and only got 42 out of 100 in a practice exam

last week. You don't need to worry about Physics – he ⁵ _____

pass easily. His French is getting better – he ⁶ _____ get a

distinction, but he ⁷ _____ at least pass.

May and *Might* 2 – speculations and warnings

1 Speculating about what's happening

(See also p. 23.)

'They can't *be . . . ing*, can they? They *might/may be . . . ing.*'
(= IT'S SURELY NOT POSSIBLE THEY ARE . . .; PERHAPS THEY ARE . . .)

When Mr and Mrs Wilson were in Italy, they went to the cinema
– but they couldn't understand the dialogue very well! Look at
the pictures (scenes from the film) and complete their
conversation with *can/can't/might/may*:

1 'Those men ___can't be___ cleaning windows, _____ they?

It's night!' 'No, they _____ . They _____

robbers, I suppose.'

2 'Look at the girl. I thought she was laughing, but she

_____ be, _____ she?' 'She _____ .

crying because she's afraid of those men.'

3 'What are those people doing? I thought they were having a

rest, but they _____ be, _____ they? The police

seem to be angry with them.' 'I think they _____

protesting about something.'

2 Warnings!

Here is some advice that the travel agent gave Mr Wilson before
he went to a foreign country. Complete it with *may/might (not)*
+ phrases from the list:

get ill	stop	have to pay a lot
ask	be a lot of traffic	have been
		washed

1 You'd better leave for the airport early – there___*may/might be a lot of traffic.*___ .

2 Don't drink water from the taps – you _____ .

3 Don't eat salad in restaurants – it _____ properly.

4 You'd better take out medical insurance – you _____ otherwise.

5 Mind how you cross the road when you're there – the traffic _____
even if the lights are red.

6 Take your passport everywhere with you – the police _____
to see it.

3 Speculating about the past – *may have, might have*

Rewrite these sentences using *may/might (not)* or *may/might (not) have*, instead of *perhaps, it's possible* and *maybe*. (Remember that the only difference between *may* and *might* is that *might* is weaker.)

1 Perhaps they have forgotten where we live.
 They may have forgotten where we live.

2 It's possible they've lost our address.

 _____

3 There's a possibility that they didn't get our invitation.

 _____

4 Or maybe they thought it said Thursday, not Tuesday.

 _____

5 It's possible their car has broken down.

 _____

6 Perhaps they have been held up by a traffic jam in the centre.

 _____

7 Or maybe someone telephoned them when they were leaving.

 _____

4 *May/might (not) + be . . . ing or have been . . . ing?*

What reasons might there be for the situations in the pictures?

Perhaps he/she/they:
- was trying to carry too much
- have been walking for a long time
- wasn't holding it properly
- is going for a swim
- aren't wearing comfortable shoes
- was going too fast

1 He may/might have been going too fast.

 Or he _____

2 She _____

 Or she _____

3 They _____

 Or they _____

14 *Might have, Could have* and *Couldn't have*

Mrs Wilson is reading an exciting murder story. She is trying to explain to her husband the plot so far, and to deduce who committed the crime. Complete the blanks, using *might have* or *could have* (= IT'S POSSIBLE), and *couldn't have* (= IT'S NOT POSSIBLE):

'Lord Moneybags has been murdered – he was shot in the library just before dinner. Jenkins, the butler, says he ran into the library as soon as he heard the shot, and found Lord Moneybags dead on the floor. There was nobody else in the room, and the window was shut. Lord Moneybags' own gun was in his hand, and there were no other fingerprints on it.'

'Well, he ¹ _might have_ committed suicide, ² _mightn't he_ ?'

'No, the detective says he ³_____ done that, because he had no reason.'

'But he ⁴_____ had money problems that nobody else knew of.'

'Yes, I suppose he ⁵_____ , but Inspector North is sure he was murdered.'

'Who are the suspects, then?'

'Well, there were six other people in Moneybags Hall that evening, and they all have an alibi for the time of the murder. But any of them ⁶_____ committed the crime, because they all had a motive!'

	Suspects	Alibi	Possible motive
	Lady Moneybags (his wife)	She was upstairs, dressing for dinner.	They had had violent quarrels lately. She thought he was interested in Madeleine.
	Monty, his son	He was helping Madeleine lay the dinner table.	He needs money urgently, to pay gambling debts.
	Madeleine, the maid	She was laying the table for dinner (with Monty).	Monty says he wants to marry her, but his father won't allow it.
	Clara (Lord M.'s mad sister)	She was walking round the garden, singing.	She believes her brother is very bad.
	Mrs Jones, the cook	She was frying chips in the kitchen.	She has secretly loved Lord M. for 25 years, but he ignores her.
	Jenkins, the butler	He was polishing the mirror in the hall.	Lord M. has promised him some money when he dies – Jenkins has debts, too!

Moneybags Hall – Ground Floor

'Lady Moneybags [7]_____ killed him, because she was upstairs. Jenkins was in the hall, so it [8]_____ been him, [9]_____ it? Monty [10]_____ done it, because he was with Madeleine – and she was with him, so she [11]_____ done it either, [12]_____ she? But, wait a moment, they [13]_____ planned it together, [14]_____ they?'

'Well, I'm not reading the book, so I don't really know, but what about Clara? She's mad, so she [15]_____ done it. She [16]_____ climbed through the window from the garden, still singing! Or the cook [17]_____ left her chips for a moment and gone to the library, I suppose. But then Jenkins would have seen her ...... but, of course, he had a motive, too! He and the cook [18]_____ done it together.'

'It's difficult, isn't it. It [19]_____ any of them. I'd better read some more.'

WELL? WHO DO YOU THINK IT [20]_____ BEEN? INSPECTOR NORTH SOON DISCOVERS AN IMPORTANT CLUE – MRS WILSON TELLS HER HUSBAND ABOUT IT ON PAGE 39!

15 *Must* – necessity

1 *Must* and *mustn't* are used for GENERAL NECESSITY – things which it is **absolutely necessary to do**, or **not to do** (see also p. 36). When you learn to drive, there are some important things to remember. Sort out the jumbled list, and begin each one with *You must* or *You mustn't*:

look in	the speed limit
stop	before you turn
wear	at a red light
overtake	your seatbelt
signal	on a bend
go faster than	your mirror

1 *You must look in your mirror.*
2 _____
3 _____
4 _____
5 _____
6 _____

2 Write five things students *must* or *mustn't* do when they take an exam:

1 *They must arrive on time.*
2 _____
3 _____
4 _____
5 _____

3 In speech, we often say things like *Don't leave the door open!*, but a formal notice would probably say:

> THIS DOOR MUST NOT BE LEFT OPEN

What notices would you write about these things? – use *must be* or *must not be*.

1 Return the key after use.
   The key must be returned after use.

2 Don't keep books for more than two weeks.
   Books _____

3 Students are not allowed to use this computer.
   This computer _____
   _____

4 Turn off all lights by midnight.
   All lights _____
   _____

5 Leave your bag with the librarian.
   Bags _____

6 It is forbidden to make copies without permission.
   Copies _____
   _____

4 **Must, Mustn't, Needn't**

You *must* ...	It's NECESSARY
You *mustn't* ...	It's FORBIDDEN
You *needn't* ...	It's NOT NECESSARY

When you arrive in Britain, there are plenty of regulations to worry about. There are things that are NECESSARY, UNNECESSARY, or FORBIDDEN. Use the modals above to complete the following statements:

1 _You mustn't_ bring animals into Britain.

2 _____ have a passport.

3 _____ have a visa, if you want to stay a long time.

4 _____ have a visa if you are from an EEC (Common Market) country.

5 _____ declare any restricted goods at the customs.

6 _____ declare cigarettes up to a certain limit.

7 _____ take guns into Britain.

8 _____ drive on the left.

9 _____ stop at pedestrian crossings unless someone is on them.

10 _____ use the horn on your car except in an emergency.

5

Mrs Wilson is telling her husband what has been happening. Write his reactions, using *must, mustn't* or *needn't* + one of these expressions, and a tag question:

buy anything too expensive   be paid immediately   do any housework   make him change his mind   be stopped

1 Stephen has announced that he is going to drop out of school.
   We must make him change his mind, mustn't we?

2 They have been invited to a wedding, and will have to buy a present.
   We _____ , _____ ?

3 The owners of the house across the road want to open a gambling club.
   They _____ , _____ ?

4 The doctor has told Gran to rest completely.
   She _____ , _____ ?

5 The telephone bill has arrived – the final date for payment is in two weeks.
   It _____ , _____ ?

16 *Must* and *Have to*

Must	strong necessity for present or future:
	e.g. Everyone *must* be back here by 6 o'clock.
	   = I SAY IT IS NECESSARY THAT . . . .
	   or I ORDER/URGE EVERYONE . . .
	   or I AGREE WITH THE RULE THAT SAYS IT IS NECESSARY FOR EVERYONE . . .

Mustn't	prohibition – the speaker himself forbids: e.g. You *mustn't* do that again. = I ORDER YOU NOT TO DO THAT AGAIN. or states a prohibition which he supports: e.g. The police *mustn't* use guns except in self-defence. (*Can't* – see p. 24 – is less strong. The speaker is stating a fact, as with *have to*)

Have to	necessity – the speaker is not *ordering* or openly supporting an order (as with *must*). He is simply stating a fact:
	e.g. (present) Everyone *has to* fill this form in.
	   = IT IS NECESSARY . . .
	   (future) You *will have to* wait for three hours at Rome Airport.
	   = IT WILL BE NECESSARY . . .

1 Complete the sentences, using *must, mustn't, have to* or *will have to*:

1 Julie, trying to train her dog: You _____*must*_____ sit when I tell you to!

2 The teacher who is invigilating Stephen's exam:

   You _____ try to talk to each other during the exam.

3 The doctor to a nurse, about a patient with a bad heart:

   He _____ stay in bed for several weeks, and _____ talk too much.

4 Mr Wilson phones his wife at 6 pm:

   I'm afraid I'm going to be late – I _____ finish some letters.

5 The immigration officer notices that a traveller hasn't signed his new passport:

   You _____ sign it as soon as you get it.

6 Mr Wilson explains why he is taking a pill:

   I _____ take these pills for my blood pressure.

7 Mrs Wilson is offering more cake to a guest at a tea party:

   You _____ have some more cake.

8 Stephen has hurt his knee playing football:

   The doctor says I _____ play for three weeks.

Don't have to	= IT'S NOT NECESSARY (The meaning is more or less the same as *needn't* – see p. 35 – but slightly more emphatic)
e.g. You can go if you want, but you *don't have to*. (= YOU ARE NOT OBLIGED TO)	

2 What else in Britain is NECESSARY, FORBIDDEN, or UNNECESSARY?
Complete the blanks with *must, mustn't* or *don't have to*:

1 If you are ill, and the doctor comes to see you, you **don't have to** pay him.

2 If the police stop you for a motoring offence, you ＿＿＿＿＿＿ offer them money.

3 You ＿＿＿＿＿＿ carry your driving licence with you.

4 You ＿＿＿＿＿＿ have a ticket when you travel on the London Underground.

5 If the police arrest you, you ＿＿＿＿＿＿ make a statement.

6 If you are a cyclist, you ＿＿＿＿＿＿ ride on the pavement.

7 British citizens ＿＿＿＿＿＿ vote when there is an election.

3 **Necessity in the past**

I *had to* pay £5 to get in!
(It *was* NECESSARY for me to pay)

You *needn't have* paid anything!
(You *paid*, but it WASN'T NECESSARY to pay)

I showed my student's card, and *didn't have to* pay to get in.
(I *didn't pay*, because it WASN'T NECESSARY for me to pay)

Fill the blanks with *had to, didn't have to*, or *needn't have*, and any other words that may be necessary:

Carla and Alev had a class at 9 o'clock. Carla left at 8.30 and Alev left at 8.50.

Alev [1] **had to** run all the way, while Carla [2]＿＿＿＿

hurry at all. Actually, Alev [3]＿＿＿＿＿＿ , as the teacher

was 10 minutes late! At lunchtime, they went to a cafeteria.

There was a long queue, and they were late back for the

afternoon class. 'We [4]＿＿＿＿＿＿ wait for ages to be

served', Carla explained. 'You [5]＿＿＿＿＿＿ at all,'

another student said. 'I went to that new cafeteria in the square,

and [6]＿＿＿＿＿＿ wait more than a minute.'

17 *Must* – drawing conclusions

You *must* be our new neighbours! (= MY CONCLUSION IS THAT YOU ARE OUR NEW NEIGBOURS.)

For conclusions about the FUTURE we normally use *bound to*, if the subject is a person:

He's *bound to* come soon. ('He must come soon' is **possible**, but it might mean 'I have ordered him to come soon')

Can't is the opposite of *must* with this meaning:
Their story *can't* be true. (= MY CONCLUSION IS THAT THEIR STORY IS NOT TRUE) – see p. 23.

1 Complete these dialogues with *must, can't* or *is/are bound to*:

'Ah, this ¹_____ **must** _____ be the dress I ordered!'

'Oh no! There ²_____ be a mistake.

This ³_____ be mine. I asked for a red one.'

'Never mind, they're ⁴_____ change it if you ask.'

'Stephen, you ⁵_____ seriously want to drop out of school, surely? You ⁶_____ be completely crazy!

You ⁷_____ regret it in the future.

There ⁸_____ be some way I can change your mind!'

2 **Must/can't be . . .-ing**

Fill the blanks, using a modal and the PRESENT CONTINUOUS form of these verbs (+ a tag question, where required):

come / work / go / start

'The Wilsons ¹ **can't be coming, can they?**

Oh, they ²_____ _____ . George ³_____ _____

_____ late, that's all. They'll be here soon.'

'I don't remember this road at all. We ⁴_____ _____

_____ the right way, ⁵_____ _____ ?'

'No, we ⁶_____ . We should have brought a map.

Bill and Brenda ⁷_____ _____ _____ to

worry by now, ⁸_____ _____ ?'

3 *Must have* – conclusions about the past

Madeleine *must have* left it there!
She *couldn't have* noticed it. (See p. 23.)

Mrs Wilson has read a bit more of her book – Inspector North has found a clue: a long yellow hair on the library floor! Madeleine, the maid, has long yellow hair.... Complete the conversation with *must have* or *couldn't have*:

MRS WILSON: 'I knew it all the time. Madeleine ¹ _**must have**_ killed him. And Monty ² _____

_____ helped her. But they ³ _____ _____ planned it very well,

⁴ _____ they, because they left such an important clue!'

MR WILSON: 'I don't agree. Those two ⁵ _____ _____ committed the murder. That would

be too obvious for a mystery story. I still think it ⁶ _____ _____ been Jenkins.

He had a good motive. Madeleine's hair ⁷ _____ _____ fallen out earlier,

when she was cleaning the library.'

DON'T MISS THE NEXT AMAZING DEVELOPMENT, ON PAGE 56!

4 Conclusions about causes of a present situation

Use the table to suggest an explanation for each situation (for *can't have* see p. 23).

It They	must have been can't have been	blown down made given washed watered broken	enough to eat together with blue clothes very well at the factory by the wind for a long time by children throwing stones

1 A new electric toy has already gone wrong.

   It can't have been made very well at the factory.

2 Some house plants are dying.

   _____

3 The windows of an empty house are all broken.

   _____

4 Some pet fish have died.

   _____

5 A tree has fallen across the road.

   _____

6 Your white shirt has turned blue!

   _____

18 Modals + *Have to* and *Be able to*

1 Computers *will be able to* do everything for us!

Stephen's grandmother is not very impressed by all this talk of computers, so he tries to explain their possibilities to her. Complete the spaces with *will, 'll* or *won't*:

STEPHEN: Just think, in a few years' time, you ¹ __won't__ have to use money at all. You ²_____

be able to use a card everywhere, and a central computer will take care of everything.

In fact you probably ³_____ have to go out of your house at all! For example,

you ⁴_____ have to go to the library to get out a book. You ⁵_____ be able to

link your computer to a 'central library', and read anything you want on your screen.

GRAN: OK, Stephen, but what shall I do if I want to read in bed? I ⁶_____ be able to take the

computer with me, ⁷_____ I! I think I'd rather have books!

STEPHEN: Oh Gran, I ⁸_____ never be able to convince you, ⁹_____ I?

2 What else is CERTAIN, PROBABLE, or POSSIBLE in the future, thanks to computers?

Rewrite the sentences. Use each of the following once: *will, won't, shouldn't, may* followed by *be able to/have to*.

1 Perhaps it will be possible for us to translate instantly by pressing a button.

   We ___*may be able to*___ translate instantly by pressing a button.

2 Then it won't be necessary for people to study languages at school.

   Then people _____ study languages at school.

3 Accurate weather forecasts will be easy for meteorologists.

   Meteorologists _____ forecast the weather accurately.

4 Perhaps it will even be possible for scientists to control the world's climate.

   Scientists _____ even _____ control the world's climate.

5 Probably it won't be necessary for students to buy so many books.

   Students _____ buy so many books.

3 Complete the dialogues using the modals in brackets at least once each:

A (*'ll/will/won't/should*)

'Oh dear, we ¹ __won't__ be able to get across, ² _____ we?'

'We ³ _____ be able to pass. We are only 2 metres 80 wide.'

'But if we don't, we ⁴ _____ have to come all the way back, ⁵ _____ we?'

B (*may/should/will*)

' ¹ _____ you be able to go, George, do you think?'

'I'm not sure. I ² _____ be able to, but I _____ have to go to Germany for a few days on business at about that time.'

Mr and Mrs J Green
request the pleasure of
Mr and Mrs G Wilson's
company at a cocktail
party on June 11th
at 6.30 p.m.

C (*will/'ll/won't/should*)

'My car needs a service. When ¹ _____ you be able to do it?'

'We're busy today, but we ² _____ be able to do it tomorrow.'

'It's still under guarantee – ³ _____ I have to pay anything?'

'You ⁴ _____ have to pay anything for the labour. You ⁵ _____ just have to pay for oil, that's all.'

D (*should/shouldn't/wouldn't*)

'Old people ¹ _____ have to queue like that to buy stamps. They ² _____ be able to sit down.'

'If they came in the afternoon they ³ _____ have to wait at all. The post office is empty then!'

19 Modals + *Have had to* and *Have been able to*

1 The Underground Cities of Cappadocia

In Cappadocia, in Central Turkey, there are two huge systems of underground tunnels and rooms. They were made by the people who lived in the region long ago, to hide when their enemies came. They often had to live in these rooms for long periods.

The city at Derinkuyu goes down for 85 metres, and has seven storeys. At Kaymakli, 10 kilometres away, only five storeys have been discovered, but it is thought that it was much larger. These cities had everything necessary to live for a long time underground: kitchens, water tanks, ventilation channels, storage rooms, wine barrels, and many separate rooms and halls connected by tunnels. In times of danger, these tunnels could be closed by big round stones.

How do you think life was for these people, when they had to spend long periods in hiding. Which of these things do you think were NECESSARY or UNNECESSARY, POSSIBLE or IMPOSSIBLE for these people? Give your opinion, using:

may/might (not) (see p. 31) must (see p. 39) couldn't (see p. 23)	+ have

1 They __must have__ *had to* control the use of water carefully.

2 They _____ *had to* go above ground sometimes, to get more food.

3 They _____ *been able to* lead a normal life.

4 They _____ *been able to* enter and leave the city by secret entrances.

5 They _____ *been able to* get rid of waste easily.

6 They _____ *had to* spend long periods without ever going above ground.

7 They _____ *been able to* bury their dead in the cities.

8 The women _____ *had to* give birth underground.

9 They _____ *been able to* make wine underground.

10 The children _____ *been able to* play easily.

11 The people _____ *had to* do a lot of things in the dark.

2 Harry Logan is well known for his interviews of famous people on television.

Tonight he is talking to Peter Michael, a popular singer. Complete the conversation by choosing the alternatives that make most sense.

HARRY: My guest tonight is that very successful young singer, Peter Michael, Peter, tell me, you ¹ { can't / (must) } { (have) / have } { (had to) / been able to } work very hard to get where you are today, I'm sure.

PETER: You're right there, Harry. It was very hard at the start. I ² { wouldn't / won't } { have / have } had to / been able to } continue as a singer if I hadn't worked as a postman during the day. Then as you know, I had a lot of luck. Without that luck, I ³ { might not / might } { have had to / have been able to } spend the rest of my life delivering letters.

HARRY: But you've had bad luck too, I know. That throat operation last year nearly ended your career, didn't it? You ⁴ { should / would } { have been able to / have had to } go back to being a postman again then!

PETER: Ha! Ha! Actually I don't think so, Harry! But if I hadn't had the operation, I probably ⁵ { might / wouldn't } { have been able to / have had to } sing properly. In fact, the doctor wasn't sure, but he thought I ⁶ { should / might } { have been able to / have had to } give up singing completely.

HARRY: But I understand you were just starting a three month tour of the States. You ⁷ { can't / must } { have had to / have been able to } cancel a lot of shows.

PETER: We were lucky – the organisers managed to get Michael Jackson to take my place. Otherwise they ⁸ { must / would } { have had to / have been able to } pay back over a million dollars in advance bookings. I'm glad I had the operation, though – you never know, I ⁹ { would / might } { have been able to / have had to } abandon the tour in the middle, and then the organisers probably ¹⁰ { wouldn't / might not } { have had to / have been able to } get someone to take my place.

HARRY: Well, Peter, let's hear a song from you now!

20 Advice, conclusions and prediction

ADVICE, or a WARNING, is often given using *should*, *ought to*, or *had better* (see Units 6 and 7). For CONCLUSIONS the modals *must* and *can't* are commonly used (see p. 38). For PREDICTIONS, we can use *will* (p. 10), or the modals of possibility: *may* and *might* (p. 29), or *could* (p. 22).

1 The objects in the pictures have something wrong with them. Write three sentences about each thing, using the modals in the boxes and the expressions in brackets (not necessarily in the same order):

1 (get worse/continue playing/have to buy a new racquet).

He <u>shouldn't continue playing</u>. { *might*

It <u>might get worse.</u> { *may*

He _____ { *shouldn't*

2 (be mended immediately/get off and walk/damage the wheel)

She _____

She _____ { *might*

The tyre _____ { *ought to*

3 (be changed/be used/cause a fire)

The wire _____ { *shouldn't*

It _____ { *should*

It _____ { *could*

4 (be sharpened/finish the job/be very blunt)

The axe _____ { *ought to*

It _____ { *must*

She _____ { *might not*

5 (be very old/be very safe/be sent to the scrapyard)

It _____ { *can't*

It _____ { *ought to*

It _____ { *must*

2 Complete the sentences with the appropriate modal, + *have* where necessary:

1 (left the window open/buy some more meat/be feeling happy)
must/'ll have to

We **must have left the window open!**

We _____

The cat _____

2 (gone to sleep/be sore tomorrow/put some cream on)
must/should/will

He _____

He _____

His back _____

3 (done it while skiing/had a car crash/be feeling fed up)
might/must

He _____

Or he _____

He _____

4 (rained very hard/spoil everyone's furniture/wait for the waters to go down)
must/'ll/'ll have to

It _____

It _____

They _____

5 (control the traffic/be working/gone on strike)
must/can't/should

The traffic lights _____

Or the bus drivers _____

The police _____

6 (left his umbrella on the bus/be in a hurry/seen him)
might/can't

He _____

Or he _____

The driver _____

21 Possibility, certainty and necessity

Possibility

Can is only used for events repeated at various times – see p. 22. (*Can't*, however, is used for any event which is thought impossible.)

May sometimes has this meaning. But more often it refers to a **specific** event at a **specific** time, like *might* (p. 29) or *could* (p. 23).

Should/ought to is used for specific events which are thought **probable** (good things only, see p. 17).

Necessity

Must = i) I BELIEVE IT'S CERTAIN (p. 38)

ii) I BELIEVE IT'S ABSOLUTELY NECESSARY (p. 34)

Have to = IT'S NECESSARY (p. 36)

Should/ought to = I BELIEVE IT'S NECESSARY OR A GOOD IDEA (p. 16)

1 In this introduction to a TV report, choose the modals (one or more) which make sense in the context:

Various reasons (^{1}*may/can*) be found for the rapid destruction of tropical forests: a particular country (^{2}*may/can*) need more land to grow food; its economy (^{3}*may/can*) depend on the export of wood; or the government (^{4}*could/may*) have begun a road or railway-building project without considering the effects on the environment. The power of multi-national companies (^{5}*can/may*) become an important factor, too. Whatever the reasons, the results are easy to predict – many types of animal (^{6}*must/have to*) disappear, and large areas of land (^{7}*should/could/must*) become deserts, as the soil is exhausted. In the long term this (^{8}*could/should/has to*) lead to a serious reduction of oxygen in the earth's atmosphere. There is no doubt that the thoughtless destruction of tropical rain forests (^{9}*must/should/has to*) be stopped before it is too late.

2 The interviewer spoke to the prime minister of a country which is destroying large areas of tropical rain forest. Rewrite his questions using one of the modals in brackets. Note that *may* is **not** used in the interrogative to mean *is it possible?*.

1 Is it impossible to save the rain forest?
(*Can't*, *Mightn't*) the rain forest be saved?

2 Isn't it possible that your country will become a desert in the future?
(*Shouldn't, Couldn't*) your country become a desert in the future?

3 Is it absolutely necessary for so much wood to be exported?
(*Must, Should*) so much wood be exported?

4 Is it possible that the new road through the forest will lead to more destruction?
(*May, Might*) the new road through the forest lead to more destruction?

3 Possibility and certainty in the past. Rewrite the opinions below, using modals:

The great crater at Tunguska, Siberia, was created in 1908 during an explosion which destroyed a large area.

1 Perhaps something from space caused it. _Something from space may/might/could have caused it._

2 It's not possible that it was caused by an ordinary meteorite.

_____

3 It's possible that a comet hit the earth.

_____

4 The explosion was certainly very powerful (judging by the damage it caused).

_____ (judging by the damage it caused).

Within a relatively short period, the dinosaurs disappeared from the earth about 55 million years ago. Why?

5 Maybe they were killed by a virus.

_____

6 It's obvious there was some great natural disaster.

_____

7 It's not possible that a minor change in climate killed them all.

_____

4 Complete the sentences with conclusions and advice which suit the pictures. Use *must, can't, may, may not, should* and *should not* once each. Add *have* as necessary.

1 It __can't have__ rained for a long time.

2 These people _____ eaten for weeks.

3 They _____ be helped as soon as possible.

4 This oil _____ come from a ship.

5 In the future, the world _____ depend on the sea for food.

6 Man _____ pollute the sea in this way.

22 Instructions and complaints

1 When the Prince of Scotland and his beautiful young wife, Princess Fiona, had their photograph taken, the Prince had some advice for the official photographer:

It really is essential that you don't let everyone see my bald patch, so it's a bad idea to have a bright light shining above my head. Princess Fiona has a tooth missing, so it's best if she's not smiling in the photo. Another problem is that she is taller than me, so I suggest that she is sitting down, and I'm standing up! Under no circumstances show her nose from the side – it's very long and I don't want anyone to know this. What else? Oh, yes! I have very big hands, so it's not a good idea for them to be included in the picture!

The photographer didn't understand very well, however, so the Prince said it all again using modals. Fill the blanks with modals. Remember, *should* = IT'S A GOOD IDEA, *must* is stronger – an ORDER.

should *shouldn't*	see p. 16
must *mustn't*	see p. 34

You really ¹ __mustn't__ let everyone see my bald patch, so there ² _____ be a bright light shining above my head. Princess Fiona ³ _____ be smiling, because of her teeth. Also, she ⁴ _____ be sitting down, and I ⁵ _____ be standing up. Now this is important: you ⁶ _____ show her nose from the side – people ⁷ _____ know that it's very long. Finally, my hands ⁸ _____ be included in the picture, as they look very big.

2 When he saw the results, he was not pleased. What really annoyed him was:

Fiona's mouth was open!
Her nose was in profile!
His bald patch was shining!
He and the Princess were looking in opposite directions!

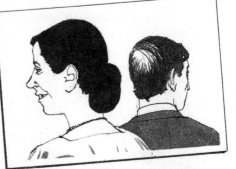

Use *should (n't)* or *ought to/ought not to* to complete the Prince's complaints:

1 My wife's mouth __should/ought to__ have been shut!

2 Her nose _____ have been shown from the side!

3 Look at my head! You _____ have switched off that light!

4 Fiona and I _____ have been looking at each other!

5 You _____ have been chosen to take the royal photograph.

3 Julie Wilson is cooking the Sunday lunch – her mother is helping her. The main course is:

'Roast lamb, with roast potatoes, cabbage, mint sauce and gravy.

She keeps asking her mother for instructions (see *shall* p. 15).

As well as giving advice and instructions (see *should* p. 16 and *had better* p. 18), her mother offers to help (see *will* p. 7).

Choose the modals (one or both) from each pair which make sense in the context:

JULIE: Mum, when (¹*will*/*shall*) I start cooking the lamb?

MUM: It depends on how big the joint is. You (²*'ll have to*/*may*) weigh it first.

JULIE: Here it is. It feels a bit hard, still. I (³*must*/*should*) have taken it out of the freezer earlier. It (⁴*must*/*should*) have been *very* well frozen!

MUM: Julie! It (⁵*must*/*should*) have been taken out last night. It (⁶*must*/*should*) be completely unfrozen before you start to cook it.

JULIE: Oh! Well, never mind, we (⁷*must*/*'ll have to*) eat a bit later than usual today, that's all. Let's see .... it weighs just over a kilo and a half.

MUM: Right. You (⁸*might*/*'ll have to*) cook it for about two hours, then. Lamb (⁹*must*/*may*) be very well cooked. You (¹⁰*'d better*/*'d rather*) put it in the oven at about 11 o'clock, then, (¹¹*wouldn't*/*hadn't*) you?

JULIE: Righto. Now what else (¹²*must I*/*will I*) do? How long (¹³*shall*/*should*) I roast the potatoes for?

MUM: Well, they have to be peeled and boiled for a short time. (¹⁴*I must do*/*I'll do*) that for you, if you like. Then you (¹⁵*have to*/*might*) put them in a hot oven for an hour, in lots of fat. When you put them in, you (¹⁶*should*/*would*) put them on the top shelf of the oven, and move the meat to a lower one. (¹⁷*Shall*/*Will*) you be able to remember all that?

JULIE: I doubt it. I (¹⁸*ought to*/*'d better*) write it down. But don't worry, Mum, (¹⁹*I'll do*/*I should do*) everything myself. Everything (²⁰*will*/*may*) be OK.

STEPHEN: Julie, when (²¹*will*/*shall*) lunch be ready? I'm starving!

Later ....

STEPHEN: Gosh, Julie! The potatoes are burnt and the lamb is raw!

JULIE: Oh dear, I (²²*should*/*must*) have made a mistake on my timetable. I (²³*should*/*must*) have cooked the meat for two hours and the potatoes for one, but I (²⁴*should*/*must*) have done it the other way round!

STEPHEN: There's an insect in the cabbage! You (²⁵*shouldn't*/*can't*) have washed it! Mum, you (²⁶*shouldn't*/*can't*) have left Julie alone in the kitchen. We (²⁷*should*/*'d better*) go out to a restaurant!

JULIE: What a good idea, Stephen! You (²⁸*can*/*could*) pay.

23 Conditionals and future

When Ernie discovered he could take a holiday in May, he and Mona went to a travel agent to make reservations. But they didn't find it easy to decide where to go.

'Morocco *would* be nice, *wouldn't* it?'
'It *might* be too hot, though, *mightn't* it.'

In the end, they wrote down the advantages and disadvantages of each place, then had a discussion at home.

	Advantages	Disadvantages
Banana Island	- nice weather - beautiful scenery	very expensive
Switzerland	- possible to ski ?	ski-ing is dangerous !
Spain	- perfect weather - good for water sports	too many people
The Lake District	- cheap - less travelling time	possibly a lot of rain always cold in May

1 Complete their discussion with:
Would/'d/wouldn't (predicting in conditional situations – including 'hidden' ones – see p. 10), *'ll/won't* (predicting the real future, or deciding/agreeing/refusing – see p. 6–7), *might* (possibility in conditionals)
Sometimes two different forms are possible.

ERNIE: How about the Lake District? If we went there, it ¹ _**wouldn't**_ cost too much, and it ² _____ take long to get there.

MONA: The trouble is the weather's so uncertain in the Lakes. It ³ _____ rain all the time we were there. It ⁴ _____ definitely be cold, and it ⁵ _____ even snow!

ERNIE: All right. Let's forget the Lakes, then. How about Spain? The weather ⁶ _____ be perfect if we went now, and we ⁷ _____ be able to go waterskiing.

MONA: The trouble with Spain is that it can get crowded. There ⁸ _____ be too many people if we went now.

ERNIE: All right, then, what about Switzerland? We ⁹ _____ still be able to ski at this time of year, ¹⁰ _____ n't we?

MONA: No, I don't think we ¹¹ _____ . It ¹² _____ be too warm for skiing. And anyway, you ¹³ _____ break your leg. You're not a very good skier.

ERNIE: Well, then, the decision seems to have been made! There's only Banana Island left on our list. We ¹⁴ _____ have to go there, ¹⁵ _____ we?

MONA: It ¹⁶ _____ be a bit expensive if we went there, but it ¹⁷ _____ certainly be nice. All right, I agree. We ¹⁸ _____ go there.

2 They went back to the travel agent. Complete their conversation, using *'d/would/'ll/will* or *might*. More than one answer may be possible.

'Good afternoon. We ¹____'d____ like to go to Banana Island for a couple of weeks!'

'Very good. When ²_____ you like to go?'

'We were thinking of May. ³_____ the weather be all right then?'

'Probably it ⁴_____ be good most of the time, but there ⁵_____ be a few showers. How were you thinking of travelling? ⁶_____ you rather fly, or go by ship?'

'We ⁷_____ have to fly, as I ⁸_____ only be able to take two weeks' holiday. How much ⁹_____ it cost if we fly?'

'Two return flights ¹⁰_____ cost you about £800, and a double room with full board in a good hotel about £100 a day.'

'Gosh! ¹¹_____ n't it be cheaper if we went by ship?'

'No, sir, if you went by sea it ¹²_____ cost about the same, in fact, and it ¹³_____ take a week longer to get there.'

'Oh well, then. That's decided. We ¹⁴_____ fly to Banana Island for two weeks in May.'

3 Match the pictures with sentences from each column to make five exchanges. Use an appropriate form of *will* or *would* in the replies.

A Shall we go to the airport by train?

B Will we get there on time?

C Can you tell me where we check in for the Banana Island's flight, please?

D Where would you like to sit?

E What shall we do till it's time to board?

a I know! We ____'ll____ have lunch!

b Oh no! We _____ miss the flight! Let's take a taxi.

c You _____ have to go to that desk over there.

d We _____ be early if there isn't a traffic jam.

e We _____ like to be near a window.

24 Getting people to do things

1 The Littles have some complaints about their hotel. Write what they said when they complained.
Use the different ways of requesting (see pages 8, 24 and 25) to show how they started by being very polite, but gradually became **more and more annoyed**.

> *Could you possibly ... Could you ... Would you ... Can you ... Will you ...*

Use *must* and *can't* in the complaints.

1 The air-conditioner won't work.

'Oh, excuse me. __Could you possibly__ send an electrician to our room? The air-conditioner

isn't working. There __must__ be something wrong with it.'

2 It wasn't possible to open the window.

'I'm afraid it's me again. We _____ open the window. It _____ be stuck.

3 The shower flooded the whole bathroom.

'Look, our bathroom is full of water – the shower _____ have been properly installed.

_____ send a plumber up as soon as possible?'

4 There was a lot of noise from below in the middle of the night.

'Look here, we _____ sleep because of the noise coming from the room below ours.

_____ tell them to stop it at once? They _____ be having a party.'

5 Next morning, Mona found a half-eaten sandwich in a drawer.

'Look here, what kind of a hotel is this? Our room _____ have been cleaned before we

arrived. _____ send someone up to clean it straightaway!'

2 **Requests with tag questions**

> 'Stop it, *will you*?' (angrily direct)
> 'You couldn't move a bit, *could you*?' (coldly polite, or sarcastic)

Which form do you think Ernie used:

1 to ask another guest at the hotel to *turn his radio down*:

_____

2 to ask a taxi-driver to *drive more carefully* (after narrowly avoiding an accident):

_____

3 to ask a small boy on the beach to *leave them in peace*: _____

4 to ask a waiter to *bring them some lunch* (after they have waited for half an hour):

_____

3 On the flight back to England, the stewardesses were busy the whole time. Some of the passengers asked for things politely, others less politely. Use:

Will you.... Would you....	Can you.... Could you....	Could you possibly...... I was wondering if you could......	+ a suitable verb

or nothing – i.e. the plain imperative (*Go away!*)

1 Ernie and Mona were very polite:

'Excuse me, ____*could you possibly bring*____ us a bottle of water and two glasses?'

2 Later, Ernie was annoyed by someone smoking in the non-smoking section. He asked the stewardess:

'Excuse me, _____ that man to stop smoking?'

3 The man who was smoking was less polite:

'_____ me a cup of coffee, love?'

4 When the stewardess asked him to stop smoking, he said:

'_____ him he can move to another seat if he doesn't like my smoke!'

5 When they were about to land, there was an announcement over the intercom:

'Ladies and gentlemen, we shall shortly be landing at Heathrow Airport.

_____ please extinguish your cigarettes and fasten your seat belts.'

4 *I/We should be grateful if you would*... is very formal, and usually only found in impersonal letters, to ask for something. When they got home. Ernie realised he had left his watch in the hotel, so he had to write to the hotel:

> Dear Sirs,
>   I am afraid that I left my watch in the bedroom when we left your hotel yesterday morning.¹_____
> send it to me as soon as possible.
>   Yours faithfully,
>   E. Little

This what the hotel wrote back to him:

> Dear Mr. Little,
> Thank you for your letter of June 2nd. Unfortunately, we have several watches in our Lost Property Department.
> ²_____ provide us with full details of the make, appearance, etc., of the watch you lost.
>   Yours sincerely,
>   J. Walker
>   (General Manager, Banana Palace Hotel)

25 General review 1

1 Mr and Mrs Wilson decided to move house. They wanted a larger
house, near a village. The first step was to talk to an estate agent.
Decide which modals make sense and are suitable in each
context (the answer may be one or both):

'(¹*May*/*can*) you help us? We (²'*ll*/'*d*) like a
house with a large garden. It
(³*mustn't*/*needn't*) be in the village, but it
(⁴*has to*/*must*) be on a bus route.
It (⁵*may*/*must*) have separate sitting and
dining rooms, and it (⁶*mustn't*/*shouldn't*) cost
more than £100,000.'
'Let's see. We have three that (⁷*can*/*might*) be
suitable. (⁸*Would*/*Should*) you like to go and
see them now?'

They didn't like the first one they looked at:

'It's too far from the village. You
(⁹*couldn't*/*wouldn't be able to*) walk to the
station in less than half an hour. You
(¹⁰*must*/*would have to*) drive there and pay
for the car park every day.'
'The house isn't in very good condition. It
(¹¹*must*/*would have to*) be redecorated. It
(¹²*can't*/*must*) have been neglected.'

The second, however, was much better:

'The agent said it's a hundred years old, but it
(¹³*can't*/*must*) have been modernised
recently. The people who lived here
(¹⁴*must*/*can't*) have been very keen on
gardening, though – the garden is a mess!'
'Yes, we (¹⁵'*d have to*/*ought to*) work hard to
make the garden look nice, but on the other
hand we (¹⁶*could*/'*d be able to*) move into the
house without redecorating.'

They also liked the third one:

'I like it, but they (¹⁷*mustn't*/*shouldn't*) have
painted the walls pink. They (¹⁸*must*/*might*)
have liked pink very much!'
'It's a nice house, but I agree we (¹⁹*shall*/'*d
have to*) change the colour of the walls. I
(²⁰*couldn't*/*can't*) decide which house I like
more. We (²¹'*ll have to*/*must*) ask the children
what they think.'

2 They went home to have a discussion with Julie and Stephen.

JULIE: (¹*Do we have to/Must we*) move? Why (²*should/can't*) we stay here?
STEPHEN: I'd (³*rather/better*) move. We (⁴*could/can*) have a bigger garden, and I (⁵*could/'d be able to*) play my guitar as loud as I liked without annoying the neighbours!
MR WILSON: I think you (⁶*would/had*) both better come with us to see the houses we liked. We (⁷*wouldn't/won't*) decide anything before that.

In the end, they all agreed on the third house. Choose suitable modals, and complete the tag questions where necessary.

STEPHEN: We'd have much more space than we have here, ⁸_____ we? There'd be no complaints from the neighbours when I play my electric guitar, ⁹_____ ?

JULIE: I like the pink walls. We (¹⁰*needn't/mustn't*) change the colour, I don't think.

MR WILSON: I'd soon get used to walking a bit further to the station, ¹¹_____ ? In fact it (¹²*can/might*) do me good, ¹³_____ !

MRS WILSON: Let's make them an offer today, George, (¹⁴*should/shall*) we?

MR WILSON: I agree. They're asking for £98,500 so we (¹⁵*may/'ll*) offer them £95,000.

Later the estate agents get a reply from the sellers of the house:

'They (¹⁶*ll/won't*) accept £95,000 – they say it's too low. But I think they (¹⁷*d/might*) accept a better offer. (¹⁸*Will/Shall*) I tell them (¹⁹*you'll offer/you must offer*) £97,000?'

'OK, we (²⁰*won't/'ll*) offer £97,000 but we (²¹*won't/'ll*) pay more.'

3 The Wilsons continue to talk about the house. Complete the remarks with sentences from the list, and add a tag question **where possible**. (Remember that it is **not** possible to say *mayn't* – see p. 5).

we may have to call an electrician
they ought to accept our offer
we'd better ask the bank for a loan
there won't be much traffic going past
it could be converted into another bedroom
we'll be able to play football in it

1 It's in a quiet road, so *there won't be much traffic going by, will there* ?

2 We've only got £80,000, so _____

3 There's a very big garden, so _____

4 There's a large attic so _____

5 The electrical system looks dangerous, so _____

6 They've been trying to sell the house for ages, so _____

26 General review 2

MONEYBAGS CASE SOLVED!
Inspector North decided to interview all the suspects separately.
Complete the dialogues with the modals in brackets. Sometimes
more than one is possible, but use each modal at least once:

A (*would/could/might*)

NORTH: You [1] __could__ have run down the stairs, shot your
husband, and run back to the bath without anyone seeing
you!

LADY M.: No, I [2]_____ n't. That [3]_____ have been
impossible. How [4]_____ I have done all that
without being seen by Jenkins?

NORTH: Ah!! Jenkins [5]_____ have helped you,
[6]_____n't he?

B (*would/must/can't/need*)

NORTH: You [1]_____ have helped Lady Moneybags to
commit the crime. You [2]_____ n't bother to tell
more lies!

JENKINS: I [3]_____ never have helped her do anything! I
[4]_____ stand her! [5]_____ you see it [6]_____
have been Monty – he was always arguing with his
father about money!

C (*should/would/could/must/can't*)

NORTH: Maud Sludge! You [1]_____ have killed your master.
You [2]_____ hide the truth any longer. You
[3]_____ n't accept the way he criticised your
cooking, [4]_____ you?

SLUDGE: It's true he was cruel to me, and I [5]_____ nave
killed the old fool. But I didn't! And you [6]_____
say I did! It [7]_____ have been that impertinent
new French maid. You [8]_____ see the way she
goes after Monty, and Lord Moneybags [9]_____ n't
agree to their marriage.

D (may/can/would/has to)

NORTH: ¹_____ you mind telling me what you were doing at the time of the murder?

MONTY: As you ²_____ recall (since I have told you before), I was teaching Madeleine how to lay the table the English way. She ³_____ do it absolutely right, you know, otherwise Mrs Sludge gets angry with her. Poor Madeleine ⁴_____ never remember whether the forks go on the left or the right! I was just showing her, when we heard the shot, and ran to the library.

E (must/'ll/could/can)

NORTH: Young lady, ¹_____ you explain to me how one of your hairs was found near the body?

MADELEINE: Certainly, it ²_____ have fallen out of my head from shock, when I saw my dear master lying dead.

F (must/'ll/could/can)

NORTH: Lady Clara, did you get on well with him?

CLARA: No, I ¹_____ n't stand him! He ²_____ pay for it, though!

NORTH: Who? Your brother?

CLARA: No, Barratt, the gardener. My brother sent him away last week. Barratt ³_____ have killed him. I saw him climb through the library window just before the shot was fired.

NORTH: Good lord! Why didn't you tell me before? He ⁴_____ still be in the house!

G (ought to/must/can't/won't)

'Good lord! The writer ¹_____ think his readers are stupid. I ²_____ read any more of *his* books!'

'You ³_____ try writing a murder story yourself. It ⁴_____ be easy!'

27 A final check

1 As you know, different modals can often mean more or less the same thing. On the other hand, one modal can often have several possible meanings. Two possible paraphrases are given after each sentence below. Decide which is the correct one.

1 Little children *can* be very noisy.
  ✓ a) Noise is a POSSIBILITY when little children are around.
  b) Making noise is a SKILL that little children have.

2 The plane *must* arrive soon.
  a) I ORDER the plane to arrive soon.
  b) I am CERTAIN that the plane will arrive soon.

3 Customers *may* leave their cars in the car park behind the shop.
  a) Customers have PERMISSION to leave their cars in the car park behind the shop.
  b) There is a POSSIBILITY that customers will leave their cars in the car park behind the shop.

4 Lady Clara *could have* committed the crime.
  a) There is a POSSIBILITY that Lady Clara committed the crime.
  b) Lady Clara had the SKILL to commit the crime.

5 Paul has a class until eight o'clock, so he *may* not get here in time for the start of the film.
  a) He does not have PERMISSION to get here in time for the start of the film.
  b) There's a POSSIBILITY he won't get here in time for the start of the film.

6 No one *can* drive faster than 30 miles an hour in towns.
  a) No one has the SKILL to drive faster than 30 miles an hour in towns.
  b) No one has PERMISSION to drive faster than 30 miles an hour in towns.

7 I *couldn't* walk until I was a year and a half old.
  a) I did not have PERMISSION to walk until I was a year and a half old.
  b) I did not learn the SKILL of walking until I was a year and a half old.

8 Stephen *should* pass his exams.
  a) It is PROBABLE that Stephen will pass his exams.
  b) Stephen has an OBLIGATION to pass his exams.

9 *Will* you answer the phone?
  a) Are you going, in the FUTURE, to answer the phone?
  b) I REQUEST that you answer the phone.

10 You *should* wear glasses.
  a) My ADVICE is that you wear glasses.
  b) There is a PROBABILITY that you will wear glasses.

11 I *couldn't* start my car this morning.
  a) I did not have PERMISSION to start my car this morning.
  b) I did not MANAGE to start my car this morning.

2 Finally (now that you are an expert on modals) have a look at these mistakes by foreign students, and explain to them what is wrong (using the modals in brackets):

A 'When I must to come?' (*must/should/can't*)

You [1] **can't** use *to* after *must*, and in questions the

modal [2]_____ go before the subject. You [3]_____ have

said: ' [4]_____ ?'

B 'Yesterday I must go to the dentist.' (*can/can't/had to/should*)

Must [1]_____ be used with a past time adverbial. It

[2]_____ only refer to the present or future. What you [3]_____

have said was: ' [4]_____ ,

C 'Now I am on holiday. I am happy because I mustn't go to school!' (*needn't/shouldn't/should/would*)

You [1]_____ have used *mustn't* here. People

[2]_____ think that you meant 'I am not allowed to go to

school.' If you mean 'It's not necessary', you [3]_____ say:

'I [4]_____ go to school.'

D 'It's getting cloudy. It can rain later, perhaps.' (*can/can't/ought to/may*)

What you [1]_____ have said, instead of *can*, is

[2]_____ . If you are talking of the possibility that a

specific event will happen in the future, you [3]_____ use

can. You [4]_____ only use *can* for general events that

happen from time to time.

E 'Don't worry, I do it for you!' (*can/can't/'ll/should*)

When you offer or promise to do something, you [1]_____

use the present simple, although you [2]_____ in some other

languages. 'I do it for you' [3]_____ only mean 'I always do it

for you.' You [4]_____ have said: 'Don't worry, I

[5]_____ .

Answer key

1 *Will* and *Would* 1 – future and reported speech (page 6)

1 1 will there be 2 there'll be 3 will there be 4 there won't be 5 There'll be 6 Won't there be 7 there'll be 8 there won't be

2 1 won't; will you; we won't 2 will; won't it; it will 3 won't; will there; there won't 4 will; won't they; they will

3 1 wouldn't be 2 would be finished 3 would be careful 4 wouldn't be

4 1 will you have 2 I'll have 3 Will you have 4 I won't have 5 I'll have 6 We'll have 7 will you have 8 I won't 9 we won't have

5 1 I'll call him 2 'll push 3 won't sink 4 'll get 5 'll post 6 'll pay 7 won't charge 8 'll give 9 won't get

2 *Will* and *Would* 2 – requesting and refusing (page 8)

1 1 would you 2 Will you 3 Would you 4 Will you

2 (*Suggestions*) 1 Would you mind not smoking here? 2 Would you mind being quiet (not talking)? 3 Would you mind closing the window?

3 1 wouldn't start 2 won't ... start 3 wouldn't ... accept 4 won't accept 5 wouldn't ... start 6 wouldn't stay 7 won't light 8 wouldn't let 9 won't move 10 wouldn't stop

3 *Will* and *Would* 3 – conditionals (page 10)

1 1 They'll 2 They'll 3 he'd 4 They'd 5 he ... wouldn't 6 Will they

2 1 'll cut; 'd cut yourself 2 'll get; would get dirty 3 won't catch; wouldn't catch their flight 4 'll burn; 'd burn herself ... touched that saucepan 5 won't go; wouldn't go to the cinema ... didn't do your homework 6 'll wake; would wake ... made a noise

3 1 would have ('d have) 2 wouldn't have 3 would 4 would have 5 wouldn't 6 would have 7 wouldn't have 8 would

4 1 wouldn't 2 would have 3 wouldn't 4 wouldn't have 5 would 6 would have 7 'd 8 wouldn't 9 would 10 wouldn't have 11 would

4 *Will* and *Would* 4 – other uses (page 12)

1 1 That'll be the postman. 2 'll be for one of the children. 3 won't have woken up yet. 4 will be getting worried. 5 'll be your great-grandmother. 6 'll have changed.

2 1 wouldn't leave his wet towel on the bed! 2 would make her bed! 3 would turn off his light! 4 wouldn't leave his muddy shoes on the carpet! 5 wouldn't spill coffee on the tablecloth! 6 would offer to wash up!

3 1 would you like to 2 Would you rather 3 'd rather 4 Would you like to 5 'd rather have 6 Would she like 7 'd rather not 8 'd rather/'d like to

4 1 like to have seen 2 rather not have 3 rather have gone 4 rather not have

5 *Shall* (page 14)

1 1 shall not 2 shall do our best to send it off 3 shall make 4 I shall not be here 5 I shall be 6 will be 7 there will not be 8 we shall be able

2 1 Shall I answer the door? 2 Shall I take your coat? 3 Shall I (we) open the window? 4 Shall I get you another glass? 5 Shall we listen to some music? 6 Shall I (we) turn on the light?

3 1 How shall I clean this pan? 2 Where shall we put these flowers? 3 How shall I sweep up this broken glass? 4 Where shall we put away the tablecloth? 5 How shall I remove these stains?

6 *Should* and *Ought to* 1 – advice and criticism (page 16)

1 (*Suggestions*) 1 You shouldn't eat so much. He ought to go on a diet. 2 You shouldn't smoke. He ought to take more care of his health. 3 You shouldn't study so hard. He ought to relax more.

4 *Will* and *Would* 4 *(continued)*

4 1 should have 2 shouldn't (ought not to) have tried 3 shouldn't (ought not to) have started booing 4 should (ought to) have been given 5 should (ought to) have tried 6 should (ought to) have been watching 7 shouldn't (ought not to) have been

5 1 shouldn't/ought not to have 2 should/ought to 3 shouldn't/ought not to 4 should/ought to 5 shouldn't/ought not to have 6 should/ought to have

7 *Should* and *Ought to* 2 – contrasted with *had better*; future probability (page 18)

1 1 'd better 2 'd better 3 'd better not 4 'd better not 5 'd better 6 'd better

2 A 1 should/ought to have 2 should/ought to have 3 shouldn't/ought not to have 4 shouldn't/ought not to have 5 should/ought 6 'd better 7 hadn't B 1 shouldn't have/ought not to have 2 should/ought they 3 should/ought to have 4 should/ought to 5 should/ought to/'d better 6 shouldn't/oughtn't/hadn't C 1 shouldn't/ought not to have 2 should/ought we 3 'd better not 4 had 5 shouldn't/ought not to 6 should/ought to 7 shouldn't/oughtn't they

3 1 should 2 shouldn't/ought not to 3 should/ought to 4 shouldn't/oughtn't 5 should/ought to 6 should/ought to 7 shouldn't/ought not to

8 *Can* and *Could* 1 – skill and achievement (page 20)

1 1 can ... can't 2 can ... quite well ... can 3 can't ... very well ... can ... quite well 4 can ... quite well ... can't 5 (e.g.) Portuguese ... (e.g.) read 6 can read ... can understand

3 1 can't ... he'll be able to 2 can't ... 'll be able 3 can ... 'll be able to 4 won't be able to ... 'll be able to type

4 1 was able to 2 couldn't 3 was able to 4 couldn't 5 were able to 6 could

[9] *Can* and *Could* 2 – possibility (page 22)

[1] 1 can be dangerous 2 can get cool 3 could take over an hour 4 could be cuts

[2] 1 can 2 could 3 can 4 could 5 can 6 could

[3] 1 could 2 can't 3 could 4 can't/couldn't 5 couldn't 6 could 7 couldn't

[4] A 1 could have 2 couldn't have 3 could have been 4 couldn't it B 1 could have 2 can't/couldn't have been 3 Could ... have 4 could have been

[10] *Can* and *Could* 3 – permission and requests (page 24)

[1] 1 can't smoke 2 can't enter (go in) 3 can ... go in (enter) 4 can't go can turn (go) left 5 can wash ... you can't 6 can ... can't

[2] 1 could you 2 Can you 3 Could you tell 4 Could I 5 Could you 6 Can I 7 Could I (we)

[3] (*Suggestions*) 1 Could I possibly leave the office an hour earlier than usual? 2 You couldn't possibly lend me your guitar for the evening, could you? 3 I was wondering if you could help me carry a cupboard upstairs. 4 Could you move your car? 5 I was wondering if we could leave early today? 6 Do you think you could do some shopping for me if you have time? 7 Do you think I could look at your newspaper? 8 I couldn't possibly use your phone, could I? 9 Could you possibly give me a lift into town? 10 Can I pay my bill?

[11] *Could* – unreal and conditional uses (page 26)

[1] 1 I could eat a kilo of rice! 2 I could drink eight bottles of lemonade. 3 I could sleep for 24 hours. 4 I could melt. 5 could look at them all day. 6 could have drunk eight bottles of lemonade. 7 could have slept for 24 hours. 8 could have melted. 9 could have looked at them all day.

[2] 1 I wish I could eat cakes. 2 I wish I could find my key. 3 I wish we could use dictionaries. 4 I wish I could afford a new car. 5 I wish I could get a job. 6 I wish we could understand the instructions.

[3] (*Suggestions*) 1 You could have set fire to yourself. 2 The house could have been burnt down. 3 It could have broken. 4 We could have had an accident.

[4] 1 Couldn't you have got a lift? I could have, but nobody stopped. 2 Surely you could have phoned a garage? No, I couldn't, because there was no phone nearby. 3 Couldn't you have walked to the next village? No, I couldn't, because (I could have, but) it was too far. 4 Surely you could have changed the wheel yourself! No, I couldn't, because (I could have, but) I didn't have any tools.

[12] *May* and *Might* 1 – permission and possibility (page 28)

[1] (*Suggestions*) 1 I was wondering if I might have the afternoon off work. 2 May I make a suggestion? 3 I was wondering if I might visit the pilot's cabin. 4 May I use the phone? 5 Do you think I might borrow your ladder?

[2] 1 may not be 2 may not 3 may not be 4 may ... be booked 5 may not smoke in the classrooms

[3] 1 Her train may be late. 2 She may not know the way. 3 She might think it's on another day. 4 There may be a traffic jam. 5 She may feel the salary is too low. 6 She might not want the job after all. 7 She may not be feeling well today. 8 She might have a good reason.

[4] 1 should 2 may 3 might 4 may not 5 should 6 may not 7 should

[13] *May* and *Might* 2 – speculations and warnings (page 30)

[1] 1 can't be ... can ... can't ... may/might be 2 can't ... can ... may/might be 3 can't ... can ... may/might be

[2] 1 may/might be a lot of traffic. 2 might get ill. 3 might/may not have been washed 4 might have to pay a lot 5 may/might not stop 6 might/may ask

[3]

1 They may have forgotten where we live. 2 They may/might have lost our address. 3 They might/may not have got our invitation. 4 They may/might have thought it said Thursday, not Tuesday. 5 Their car may/might have broken down. 6 They may/might have been held up by a traffic jam in the centre. 7 Someone may/might have telephoned them when they were about to leave.

[4]

1 may/might have been going too fast ... might/may be going for a swim. 2 might/may not have been holding it properly ... may/might have been trying to carry too much 3 may/might have been walking for a long time .... might not be wearing comfortable shoes.

[14] *Might have, Could have* and *Couldn't have* (page 32)

1 might have 2 mightn't he? 3 couldn't have 4 might/could have 5 might/could have 6 could/might have 7 couldn't have 8 could/might have 9 couldn't/mightn't 10 couldn't have 11 couldn't have 12 could 13 could/might have 14 couldn't/mightn't 15 might/could have 16 might/could have 17 could/might have 18 might/could have 19 could/might have been 20 could/might have

[15] *Must* – necessity (page 34)

[1] 1 You must look in your mirror. 2 You must stop at a red light. 3 You must wear your seatbelt. 4 You mustn't overtake on a bend. 5 You must signal before you turn. 6 You mustn't go faster than the speed limit.

[2] (*Suggestions*) 1 They must arrive on time. 2 They mustn't talk. 3 They must read the questions carefully. 4 They must bring a pen. 5 They mustn't try to see what other students are writing.

[3] 1 The key must be returned after use. 2 must not be kept for more than two weeks. 3 must not be used by students. 4 must be turned off by midnight. 5 must be left with the librarian. 6 must not be made without permission.

4 1 You mustn't   2 You must   3 You must   4 You needn't   5 You must   6 You needn't   7 You mustn't   8 You must   9 You needn't   10 You mustn't

5 1 We must make him change his mind, mustn't we?   2 needn't buy anything too expensive, need we?   3 must be stopped, mustn't they?   4 mustn't do any housework, must she?   5 needn't be paid immediately, need it?

16 *Must* and *Have to* (page 36)

1 1 must   2 mustn't   3 'll have to/must . . . mustn't   4 have to/must   5 have to   6 have to   7 must   8 mustn't

2 1 don't have to   2 mustn't   3 don't have to   4 must   5 don't have to   6 mustn't   7 don't have to

3 1 had to   2 didn't have to   3 needn't have hurried (run)   4 had to   5 needn't have waited   6 didn't have to

17 *Must* – drawing conclusions (page 38)

1 1 must   2 must   3 can't   4 bound to   5 can't   6 must   7 're bound to   8 must

2 1 can't be coming, can they?   2 must be   3 must be working   4 can't be going   5 can we   6 can't   7 must be starting   8 mustn't they

3 1 must have   2 must have   3 couldn't have   4 could   5 couldn't have   6 must have   7 must have

4 1 It can't have been made very well at the factory.   2 They can't have been watered for a long time.   3 They must have been broken by children throwing stones.   4 They can't have been given enough to eat.   5 It must have been blown down by the wind.   6 It must have been washed together with blue clothes.

18 Modals + *Have to* and *Be able to* (page 40)

1 1 won't   2 'll   3 won't   4 won't   5 'll   6 won't   7 will   8 'll   9 will

2 1 may be able to   2 won't have to   3 will be able to   4 may . . . be able to   5 shouldn't have to

3 A 1 won't   2 will   3 should   4 'll   5 won't   B 1 Will   2 should   3 may   C 1 will   2 should   3 will   4 won't   5 'll   D 1 shouldn't   2 should   3 wouldn't

19 Modals + *Have had to* and *Have been able to* (page 42)

1 (*Suggestions*) 1 must have   2 must have   3 couldn't have   4 may have   5 couldn't have   6 may have   7 couldn't have   8 must have   9 may have   10 couldn't have   11 must have

2 1 must have had to   2 wouldn't have been able to   3 might have had to   4 would have had to   5 wouldn't have been able to   6 might have had to   7 must have had to   8 would have had to   9 might have had to   10 wouldn't have been able to

20 Advice, conclusions and prediction (page 44)

1 1 shouldn't continue playing; might get worse; may have to buy a new racquet   2 ought to get off and walk; might damage the wheel; ought to be mended immediately   3 should be changed; shouldn't be used; could cause a fire   4 must be very blunt; ought to be sharpened; might not finish the job   5 must be very old; can't be very safe; ought to be sent to the scrapyard

2 1 must have left the window open; 'll have to buy some more meat; must be feeling happy   2 must have gone to sleep; should have put some cream on; will be sore tomorrow   3 might have done it while skiing; might have had a car crash; must be feeling fed up   4 must have rained very hard; 'll spoil everyone's furniture; 'll have to wait for the waters to go down   5 can't be working; must have gone on strike; should control the traffic   6 might have left his umbrella on the bus; might be in a hurry; can't have seen him

21 Possibility, certainty and necessity (page 46)

1 1 can/may   2 may   3 may   4 may/could   5 can/may   6 must   7 could/must   8 could   9 must/should/has to

2 1 Can't   2 Couldn't   3 Must   4 Might

3 1 Something from space might/may/could have caused it.   2 It couldn't/can't have been caused by an ordinary meteorite.   3 A comet may/might/could have hit the earth.   4 The explosion must have been very powerful.   5 They might/may/could have been killed by a virus.   6 There must have been some great natural disaster.   7 A minor change in the climate couldn't/can't have killed them all.

4 1 can't have   2 may not have   3 should   4 must have   5 may   6 should not

22 Instructions and complaints (page 48)

1 1 mustn't   2 shouldn't   3 shouldn't   4 should   5 should   6 mustn't   7 mustn't   8 shouldn't

2 1 should/ought to   2 shouldn't/ought not to   3 should/ought to   4 should/ought to   5 shouldn't/ought not to

3 1 shall (note that *will* is possible in some dialects)   2 'll have to   3 should   4 must   5 should   6 should/must   7 'll have to/must   8 'll have to   9 must   10 'd better   11 hadn't   12 must I   13 should/shall   14 I'll do   15 have to   16 should   17 Will   18 'd better/ought to   19 I'll do   20 will   21 will   22 must   23 should   24 must   25 can't   26 shouldn't   27 'd better   28 can

23 Conditionals and future (page 50)

1 1 wouldn't   2 wouldn't   3 might   4 would   5 might   6 would   7 'd/might   8 might/'d   9 'd/might   10 would/might   11 would   12 'd/would   13 might   14 'll   15 won't   16 might/'d/would   17 'd/would   18 'll

2 1 'd   2 would   3 Will/Would   4 'll/will   5 might/'ll   6 Would   7 'll   8 'll   9 will   10 will/would   11 Would   12 'd/would   13 'd/would   14 'll

3 Picture 1 – A – b Oh no! We'd miss the flight! Let's take a taxi.
Picture 2 – B – d We'll be early if there isn't a traffic jam.
Picture 3 – C – c You'll have to go to that desk over there.
Picture 4 – D – e We'd like to be near a window.
Picture 5 – E – a I know! We'll have lunch.

24 Getting people to do things (page 52)

1
1 Could you possibly ... must
2 can't ... must 3 can't ... Would
you 4 can't ... Can you ...
must 5 can't ... Will you

2
(*Suggestions*) 1 You couldn't turn
your radio down, could you?
2 Drive more carefully, will you?
3 Leave us in peace, will you?
4 You couldn't bring us some lunch,
could you?

3
(*Suggestions*) 1 could you possibly
bring 2 I was wondering if you
could ask 3 Will you get (*or* Get
...) 4 Will you tell (*or* Tell ...)
5 Would you/Will you (*or* Please
extinguish ...)

4
1 I should be grateful if you would
2 I should be grateful if you would

25 General review 1 (page 54)

1
1 Can 2 'd 3 needn't
4 must/has to 5 must'
6 shouldn't/mustn't 7 might
8 Would 9 couldn't/wouldn't be
able to 10 would have to
11 would have to 12 must
13 must 14 can't 15 'd have to
16 could/'d be able to 17 shouldn't
18 must 19 'd have to 20 can't
21 'll have to/must

2
1 Do we have to/Must we 2 can't
3 rather 4 could 5 could/'d be
able to 6 had 7 won't
8 wouldn't 9 would there
10 needn't 11 wouldn't I
12 might 13 mightn't it 14 shall
15 'll 16 won't 17 'd/might
18 Shall 19 you'll offer 20 'll
21 won't

3
1 there won't be much traffic going
by, will there? 2 we'd better ask the
bank for a loan, hadn't we? 3 we'll
be able to play football in it, won't
we? 4 it could be converted into
another bedroom, couldn't it? 5 we
may have to call an electrician.
6 they ought to accept our offer,
oughtn't they?

26 General review 2 (page 56)

A 1 could 2 could 3 would
4 could 5 might/could
6 might/could B 1 must 2 need
3 would 4 can't 5 Can't 6 must
C 1 must 2 can't 3 could
4 could 5 should/could 6 can't
7 must 8 should 9 would
D 1 Would 2 may 3 has to
4 can E 1 can 2 must
F 1 could 2 'll 3 must
4 must/'ll/could G 1 must
2 won't 3 ought to 4 can't

27 A final check (page 58)

1
1 a 2 b 3 a 4 a 5 b 6 b
7 b 8 a 9 b 10 a 11 b

2
A 1 can't 2 must 3 should
4 When must I come? B 1 can't
2 can 3 should 4 Yesterday I had
to go to the dentist. C 1 shouldn't
2 would 3 should 4 needn't
D 1 ought to 2 may 3 can't
4 can E 1 can't 2 can 3 can
4 should 5 'll do it for you